THE
CHANGE
AGENT

THE
CHANGE
AGENT

LEE GROSSMAN

A DIVISION OF AMERICAN MANAGEMENT ASSOCIATIONS

Library of Congress Cataloging in Publication Data

Grossman, Lee.
    The change agent.

    Includes bibliographical references.
    1. Organizational change. I. Title.
HD38.G762 1975   658.4'06   74-4744
ISBN 0-8144-5364-3

First Printing

CONTENTS

V
SELLING CHANGE

I

THE CASE FOR CHANGE AGENTS

MEN, ORGANIZATIONS, AND CHANGE

Man has always had to cope with change in some form, but the disturbing feature of change today is that it's occurring so rapidly that both people and organizations are uncomfortable with it. Change is good but too rapid a rate of change has a negative effect on an organization. Some organizations have experienced changes so traumatic that many of their key people have gone into organizational shock and have been unable to adapt. They remain in shock until the changes are digested and absorbed or rejected and abandoned. In either case, the recovery period is painfully slow, and some organizations never recover completely. Once-capable people can often be found waiting in the offices of employment agencies, victims of drastic change. Those in a position to be objective often dismiss the problem as temporary. For example, economists have treated all too lightly the trauma of "temporary dislocations of the workforce" caused by automation. To the worker affected by automation, the trauma is very real indeed.

The fact that change is affecting all of us has sweeping implications for the business community. Changes in life-styles, problems associated with the generation gap, and increasing pressures from minority groups affect all people to some degree, but the businessman is affected more than most. People not only buy his products and services but supply the labor by which such products or services are produced. Thus he finds himself totally dependent on people whose traditional values and goals are subjected to the pressure of constant change.

Although the world is changing about them, many organizations try to insulate themselves and cling to a way of life rooted deep in the past. This head in the sand approach may work well for those protected from competitive pressures, but more and more organizations that maintain the ostrich posture find themselves being kicked in the rear by aggressive upstarts.

Often, little is done to accommodate the typical organization to change. Some businessmen believe that ignoring problems will make them go away. Others see the need for many changes and then start with changes which are usually too little and too late to do much good. What is needed is a better understanding of how change affects organizations and how to deal with it in the future.

Our age of increasing change has had an increasing impact on people in organizations. People work in organizations out of economic necessity. Trapped as an organization man, the individual finds himself not only a victim of broad, sweeping changes in his private life but also a victim of the changes going on within the organization. The organization, too, finds itself a victim of changes that occur within its own environment. A broad, sweeping change can have an impact at many levels of society. For example, a drastic change in a world commodity market can trigger governmental action which will affect an entire industry, and this in turn will affect each company in the industry. The final impact of the change will be on the individual both as an employee and as a consumer. Too rapid a change rate is neither natural nor good for people or organizations. Eric Hoffer, longshoreman-philosopher, stated:

> The main challenge of our age is drastic change from backwardness to modernity, from subjection to equality, from poverty to affluence, from work to leisure. These are all highly desirable changes. Yet it is becoming evident that no matter how desirable, drastic change is the most difficult and dangerous experience mankind has undergone.
>
> We are discovering that broken habits can be more painful and crippling than broken bones and that disintegrating values may have as deadly a fallout as disintegrating atoms. . . . Yet a moment's reflection will show that change such as the world has seen during the last 150 years is something wholly unprecedented and unique in mankind's experience. From the beginning of recorded history down to the end of the 18th century the way of life for the average man living in the civilized centers of the earth had remained substantially the same. . . .
>
> The end of the 18th century makes a sharp dividing line between an immemorial static world and a world of ceaseless change. It is obvious, therefore, that change is far from being as natural and matter of fact as we imagine it to be.[1]

[1] *The Temper of Our Time* (New York: Harper & Row, 1964), pp. xi–8.

The Dangers of Too Much Change

Alvin Toffler points out the dangers of change when he predicts:

> Millions of psychologically normal people will experience an abrupt collision with the future when they fall victim to tomorrow's most menacing malady—the disease of change. Unable to keep up with the supercharged pace of change, brought to the edge of breakdown by insistent demands to adapt to novelty, many will plunge into future shock. For them the future will arrive too soon.[2]

Toffler links illness with change and points out the disturbing fact that individuals who experience a great deal of change in their lives are prone to illness, and the more radical and swift the changes the more serious the illness. He continues:

> The response touched off in the human body when it is forced to adapt to change may well be accompanied by deterioration of mental functioning as well. Research findings in experimental psychology and communications theory, in management science, in human-factors engineering and space biology all point to the conclusion that man's ability to make sound decisions, to adapt, collapses when the rate at which he must make them is too fast. Whether driving a car, steering a space capsule, or solving intellectual problems, we operate most efficiently within a certain range or response speeds. When we are insufficiently stimulated by change, we grow bored and our per-

[2]*Future Shock*, from excerpts in *Playboy* magazine, February 1971, p. 94. © by Alvin Toffler.

formance deteriorates. But, by the same token, when the rate of responses demanded of us becomes too high, we also break down.[3]

Thus Toffler, in his way, is suggesting that change be maintained at a pace acceptable to people and organizations. Organizations themselves are spawning their own changes at an increasing rate, and each new development compounds the problem further. Speaking of the technological innovation cycle, Toffler points out:

> The stepped-up pace of invention, exploitation and diffusion, in turn, accelerates the whole cycle even further. For new machines or techniques are not merely a product, but a source, of fresh creative ideas. Each new machine or technique, in a sense, changes all existing machines and techniques, by permitting us to put them together into new combinations. The number of possible combinations rises exponentially as the number of new machines or techniques rises arithmetically.[4]

With the ability to develop new products and pressure to increase profits, it's no wonder we see a glut of new products in today's consumer markets. But the product glut doesn't stop there. It extends into industrial, institutional, and educational markets and wherever the novelty of innovation can lead to new sales. In organizations we see people rushing to keep abreast of the latest developments while fall-

[3] Ibid., p. 206.
[4] Ibid., p. 202.

ing further and further behind. A constantly widening assortment of innovative products, processes, equipment, supplies, materials, and services is available. Because organizations can't keep up, there is a steadily increasing information absorption gap. The overabundance of the offerings combines with human limitations to restrict the ability of organizations to react to developments which can help them. As a result, they often miss significant opportunities.

It is questionable whether people and organizations can keep up with the increasing rate of change. In Eric Hoffer's words:

> One begins to wonder whether change is at all possible; whether grown-up people can really change. And here, the story of Moses and the Exodus teaches us a sobering lesson. Moses wanted to turn a tribe of enslaved Hebrews into free men. You would think that all he would have to do is to gather the slaves and tell them that they are free. But Moses knew better.
>
> He knew that the transformation of slaves into free men was more difficult and painful than the transformation of free men into slaves. He knew that the change from slavery to freedom requires many drastic changes. First, a change in environment, a migration from one country to another. Hence, the Exodus. More vital was the endowment of the ex-slaves with a new identity and a sense of rebirth. Moses staged the drama of rebirth in the Sinai Peninsula. No playwright and no impresario had ever staged such a grandiose drama. The setting had a live volcano and the cast included the mighty Jehovah Himself.
>
> What was the denouement? Moses discovered that no migration, no drama, and no miracles could turn

slaves into free men. It cannot be done. So he led the slaves back into the desert and waited 40 years until the slave generation died and a new generation desert born and bred was ready to enter the Promised Land.[5]

Eric Hoffer's point is that so drastic a change as turning a slave into a free man is impossible. Perhaps it follows that drastic change is impossible for men in organizations. Yet organizations will have to respond if they are to survive. The implications for people in organizations are serious indeed.

For example, it's unrealistic for management to expect employees to accept broad or sweeping changes easily. Yet in many companies management expects just that and is inevitably disappointed when such changes don't go smoothly. The difficulty is very real, and managers may be forced to make drastic changes in what they do and the way that they do it. Even if management itself is flexible enough to change, what of the total organization? Large organizations with a vast amount of organizational inertia may inadvertently sabotage their own efforts to achieve necessary changes. Even the task of communicating to everyone the urgent need for change can require a staggering effort in large organizations. And the problem will probably get worse, not better. Large organizations have a way of growing larger, and their size becomes a disadvantage in an era dedicated to change.

Even scientific organizations are not more malleable. Physicist Max Planck maintained that a new scientific truth does not triumph by convincing its

[5] *Working and Thinking on the Waterfront* (New York: Harper & Row, 1969), p. 179. Copyright by Eric Hoffer.

opponents. Rather it succeeds because its opponents eventually die and a new generation grows up that is familiar with it.

While some hoped-for changes come with new generations, ever increasing change poses a problem. At the same time that the technology of modern medicine increases man's life span, nothing increases his tolerance for change. Consider the impact of the computer on people. Within a single human generation we have witnessed three generations of computers and we're well on our way to the fourth. Each succeeding generation of computers has been a radical departure from its predecessor. Many organizations had not adapted to the first generation before they were enmeshed in the second and then the third. A single human generation has had to cope with the new concepts, the new technology, the new equipment, and, most important, the impact of all this on people.

The computer has made dramatic changes in our world, perhaps as dramatic as freedom was for the slaves Moses led out of Egypt. The computer has freed employees from many burdensome tasks. But at what cost to employees? Can the people whose jobs were automated out of existence adjust to a new way of life? Have they been freed from burdensome tasks or are they doomed to spend 40 years in the desert like the slaves?

Why We Need Change Agents

Eric Hoffer contends that man is incapable of adjusting to drastic change, and Alvin Toffler predicts that

9

the increasing rate of change will cause many people to fall victim to future shock. The message for organizations is that although change is essential to survival, it has to be carefully balanced. Like a powerful drug, it can keep organizations healthy and vigorous when taken in the right amounts, but an overdose can be dangerous.

The question facing organizations is how to administer change in the proper amount, in the right places, and at the right time. The answer is the *change agent,* a key person with the expertise to administer the right changes in the proper dosages. Change agents are generalists who react to changes in the outside world and cause matching changes within the organization. They are innovators who thrive on seeing the results of their work expressed in the organization's view toward such things as profit, diversification, and social responsibility. They work for the organization's responsiveness toward its total environment. They keep the organization loose and flexible.

Within organizations, some people and departments are abler to cope with change than others. Some people, by their very nature, have a higher tolerance for change than others. They are more adaptive, more creative, more flexible. No one seems to know what makes one man more adaptable than others. Obviously, the young have a comparatively great tolerance for change. As a man matures and his habits become set, his ability to think in new ways is diminished, which explains in part why old organizations may become rigid and why they are so susceptible to shock when they are forced to change.

Organizations cannot suppress change, but through change agents they can learn to manage it. The management of change, like the management of anything else, requires skill and talent. It requires insight and understanding so that the pace is evolutionary rather than revolutionary. It requires the coordinative efforts of knowledgeable change agents to make implementation successful. The change agent knows his organization and knows how much change it can absorb. He avoids the trauma of drastic change by controlling it in bite-size chunks. He feeds the organization a chunk at a time, giving it time to digest the first before swallowing another.

To survive in a change-oriented present, change management—as practiced by change agents—has to become an integral part of the total management process. Change has become too important to leave to chance.

ANYONE CAN BE A CHANGE AGENT

Change agents are not a new idea. As Freud visualized it, the therapist's role with respect to his patient is that of change agent. The term "change agent," used by Ronald Lippett,[1] referred to an outside helper, whether person or group, who attempts

[1] *The Dynamics of Planned Change* (New York: Harcourt, Brace, 1958), p. 37.

11

to effect change in an organization. Later, Warren G. Bennis and others broadened this definition to include anyone, inside or outside the organization, who tried to effect change.[2] But in any case the change agent was a professional—often with a doctorate in some behavioral science such as psychology. Thus the early social and behavioral scientists who coined the term limited its application to skilled professionals with proper training. The change agents they described were an elite, and organizations, faced with the quickening pace of change, could not find them in sufficient number to do much good.

In recent years the study of change has broadened. Universities and institutions have researched and expanded their knowledge of change, and sophisticated concepts have evolved into practical tools of management. Douglas McGregor's classifications of Theory X and Theory Y managers, Abraham Maslow's hierarchy of needs, Frederick Herzberg's satisfiers and dissatisfiers, Robert Blake and Jane Mouton's Managerial Grid, and T-groups and sensitivity training are now familiar management techniques. Significantly, many people who use these techniques today are not the professional change agents described by Lippett or Bennis. Rather, they are homegrown varieties. To bridge the gap between supply and demand as well as between theory and practice, organizations have had to develop their own change agents.

---

[2] Warren G. Bennis, K. D. Benne, and R. Chin, eds., *The Planning of Change: Readings in the Applied Behavioral Sciences* (New York: Holt, Rinehart and Winston, 1961), p. 69.

More recent trends in the behavioral sciences have been toward organization development, which focuses on helping people and organizations to cope with change. Each summer since 1967, the National Training Laboratories has conducted organization development training for change agents from a variety of organizations. The program covers theories and strategies of change, organization diagnosis, consultation, team building, and intergroup confrontation.[3] Today's change agents are a new breed, not professional outsiders but people inside organizations who have learned from professionals.

The New Change Agents

Who are the new change agents? They've been around for some time in a variety of roles and under a multitude of titles. *The New York Times* described the evolution of industrial engineers as change agents at IBM's Endicott, New York, plant:

> Over the last two decades the industrial engineer has armed himself with a bulging bag of sophisticated tools that has permitted him to go beyond his traditional activities. . . . Industrial engineers had the responsibility for coordinating the development of the entire manufacturing process—from the planning of the factory, through definition, layout and installation of the novel production system.[4]

---

[3] Warner W. Burke, "Training Organization Development Specialists," *Professional Psychology* (Summer 1970), pp. 354–358.
[4] Reported by Stanley Klein in *The New York Times*, July 4, 1971.

Thus industrial engineers have been change agents for more than a decade. Their early efforts were limited to factories, but now they are found in offices, hospitals, and government agencies. Systems analysts are change agents. Since the fifties the Association for Systems Management has grown in number and stature. The systems concept for problem solving is now well accepted and systems people can be found in a wide variety of organizations. Controllers, accountants, and auditors have become change agents. Over the past decade the Controllership Foundation has helped shift accounting orientation from a custodial role to reactive change-oriented accounting systems.

Personnel managers and industrial relations and training people are working as change agents. Today the American Society of Training Directors is busily engaged in teaching training directors change agent techniques. Management consultants and their predecessors, the efficiency experts, have been powerful change agents. The Association of Internal Management Consultants was formed in 1971 to provide business organizations with greater in-house change capability.

Other professionals working in organizations operate as change agents although their titles disguise the fact. Production personnel, engineers, and scientists become change agents to keep up with advances in technology. Sales, marketing, and advertising personnel become change agents because they deal with rapidly changing products and markets. Wherever one looks today professionals have oriented their expertise to keep pace with our world.

Professionals have become change agents because of their professionalism and because of need, but the trend doesn't stop there. Computers have liberated lower level and middle management personnel from routine work, which gives them the time to become change agents. At one time, management experts were predicting that computers would make routine management decisions and leave managers with more time to innovate, plan, and create.[5] Recent observers have found that there *has* been a shift in the way managers spend their time. They now do less controlling and more planning and directing. And they have more time for motivating, leading, and devising new work methods.[6] Thus managers have become change agents because they have been automated out of more traditional roles.

Computers are creating change agents in other ways. Chris Argyris recently pointed out that change agents are needed to make complex computer systems work. People who are supposed to use these systems can't psychologically cope with the impact of the required changes. Argyris believes sophisticated systems cannot gain widespread acceptance until their proponents are prepared to deal with the behavioral aspects of the people they are trying to convince.[7] Thus computer enthusiasts have to be-

[5] Harold J. Leavitt and Thomas L. Whisler, "Management in the 1980's," *Harvard Business Review* (November–December 1958), pp. 41–48; and Herbert A. Simon, "The Corporation: Will It Be Managed by Machines?" *Management and Corporation: 1985* (New York: McGraw-Hill, 1961).
[6] James P. Ignizio and Robert E. Shannon, "Organization Structures in the 1980's," *Industrial Engineering* (September 1971), p. 47.
[7] "Management Information Systems: The Challenge to Rationality and Emotionality," *Management Science* (February 1971), pp. B275–B292.

come change agents if they are to succeed. If change agents are able to gain acceptance of complex computer systems because of their ability to deal with people, the lesson is clear: If Moses had had change agents to help the Hebrews adjust to their new-found freedom, the Exodus would have taken less than 40 years.

The typical organization is moving inexorably toward change agents regardless of their job titles. As a need arises and someone in the organization fills the need, a new change agent is added to the ranks. For many organizations it is a haphazard matching of need and talent.

Most organizations have failed to recognize the interrelationship between changes in their environment and their own need for internal planned mechanisms of change, and they have used change agents in limited areas to solve limited problems. The future demands a different use. If the pace of change continues to increase, we will need change agents in increasing numbers. We will need to know who they are and what they do. We will need to develop and use their talents in a more organized fashion. If organizations are to move with the times, they will have to make a conscious effort to incorporate the change agent and his concept into the very fiber of their efforts. Organizations can cope with change by broadening their base of change participation. Instead of limiting change responsibility, more people should become involved as pressures to change mount. Rather than limiting the role to an elite class, it should be popularized.

Each organization obviously has a different need

to respond to change. But there is ample evidence that organizations heavily committed to change have used the change agent concept at successively lower levels of management. The more volatile the organization, the more it should push change responsibility down to lower management. Relatively stable organizations such as government agencies may be able to operate with a fairly limited use of change agents, but they too in time will have to broaden their participation.

The Key to Productivity:
Foremen as Change Agents

Robert A. Lull, management specialist and president of Brooks International Corporation, recently wrote:

> Within American industry today, there are many complaints about inefficiency as reflected in low productivity per man hour and a decline in product quality. This is mirrored by the public in criticism about quality, cost, and service.

> Foreign manufacturers, working with cheaper labor, are often able to undercut United States prices and a trend has resulted which could some day see the giant American industrial machine retreating in the number and variety of products it manufactures. The implications for our domestic economy, to say nothing of world trade balance, are staggering and ominous.[8]

[8] Reported in the *Chicago Tribune*, November 11, 1971, sec. 2, p. 1.

According to Mr. Lull, one of the most critical problems is that the foreman or supervisor has become a cautious, beaten man. Caught between workers and management, he's lucky to survive, much less do an outstanding job. There are four and a half million supervisors and foremen in factories and offices across the country, sandwiched between 60 million workers and a million managers. The root of the problem, according to Mr. Lull, is that supervisors have to meet management's objectives while controlling a work situation fraught with difficulties. To top it off, management doesn't support them or understand their problems. As a result the typical supervisor plays it safe and strives to maintain the status quo.

Mr. Lull believes inefficiency starts at the top, is encouraged at middle management levels, and is readily adopted at the employee level where it is considered a spectator sport. His solution for inefficiency and low productivity is management education. But the problem goes deeper; it can be traced to the way organizations are structured, to misused management principles, and to the fact that foremen are not called upon to act as change agents. Because the factory foreman and the office supervisor are the links between management and work, they directly affect efficiency and productivity. In effect, a large share of the dollars spent in any company flows through their hands. They directly control workers, materials processed, and equipment. Yet the attention given these first-line supervisors is often minimal. Management neglects them because they can be neglected. The penalty for this inattention is poor productivity and unnecessarily high costs. Management should be more involved in the affairs of foremen and supervisors, but the realities of organizational life dictate otherwise.

The lack of management involvement at the foreman level is predicated on some widely accepted management principles. Typically, organizations assign authority and responsibility to managers whose place in the hierarchy is depicted in neatly arranged boxes on an organization chart. According to the principle of specialization, the occupant of each box has a job to do and has little time for those down the line, unless they aren't doing well. The principle of management by exception dictates that only exceptional things, good or bad, warrant attention. Managers seem to progress, not by working at the lower levels, but by focusing on bigger and higher causes.

This is not to suggest that we should abandon organization charts or the principles of labor specialization and exception management. What we should do is specialize and report exceptions differently. Instead of limiting a foreman's authority and responsibility, we should give him greater responsibility for changes within his sphere of activity. Instead of limiting the range of his tasks and skills, we should broaden them. The exceptions reported can then lead to productive change, and the supervisor can become a change agent. The fact that programs directed toward training foremen and supervisors to improve their skills and knowledge are being conducted by industry, associations, and universities is proof that the foreman can be effective as a change agent.

It's not an exaggeration to say the key to greater productivity is in the hands of factory foremen and office supervisors. Management may provide funds for capital equipment, but the foreman controls the ultimate efficiency of that equipment. Management may provide funds for materials but the foreman directly affects the efficient conversion of these materials into finished products. Management may provide wages but the foreman directs the activities of the people who receive these wages. A great responsibility rests on the shoulders of foremen. If they are to achieve greater productivity, management has to help them become change agents.

Learning to Think Like a Change Agent

Professor Robert L. Kahn, University of Michigan psychologist, has observed that nonsupervisory jobs in most corporations require childish rather than adult characteristics:

> As a person grows from childhood to maturity, he shows change along several lines: He moves from passivity as an infant to increasing activity as an adult; from dependence on others to relative independence; from limited behavior to a wide range of behaviors; from brief, shallow interest to deeper commitments; from a short time perspective to a longer one; from a subordinate position to one of equality among others; and from obliviousness to self-awareness and self-control.

> There is a serious and pervasive incompatability between these characteristics of the mature adult and the

20

demands of nonsupervisory jobs in most corporations. Corporate jobs require the passive acceptance of the task as defined by others, a continuing dependence on one's superiors for approval and rewards, the repetitive practice of a limited set of skills, a time perspective that is limited to the task of the moment, and the acceptance of a position subordinate in status, rewards, and decisions about one's work. . . .

The corporate structure—with its definition of job requirements, performance standards, and disregard of individual values—offers little scope for the exercise of responsibility. If responsibility means acting autonomously in accordance with one's own values, corporations tend to prevent responsible behavior on the part of most of their employees, except in the restricted sense of performing dependably on the job.[9]

Pointing to extensive research, Dr. Kahn concludes that if you want people to behave more responsibly you must give them responsibility. One way to do this is to let employees participate in change.

If all employees could think like change agents, conflict and bickering would diminish. Internal disputes somehow pale when viewed in the light of the total changes confronting the organization. A bond develops between change agents who work together for a meaningful purpose. A healthy results-oriented unity is created that frees them from the normal limitations of their jobs. Viewing the organization from a change perspective provides insight that is a

[9] From the Symposium on the American Corporation at Mid-Century. Reported in *Personnel Journal* (July 1969), pp. 558–559. Dr. Kahn was quoting in part from the work of Chris Argyris.

21

valuable motivating force in pursuing and achieving productive change.

Most organizations operate as if their people are isolated from the real world. Yet, far from being isolated, today's worker is bombarded by the media with broad, up-to-the-minute news coverage — including news of events that cast organizations in a socially irresponsible light.

In the midst of all this, employees develop ambivalent feelings about work. If work provides marginal satisfaction, the news reinforces negative attitudes. Advertising campaigns built around slogans ("we're involved") are at best delaying tactics. Employees have to become more involved in the social contribution of their organizations; they have to be given the opportunity to contribute beyond their normal tasks. Since they are not isolated from the real world, they must become partners in progress, not merely cogs in some gigantic machine. Organizations have to structure jobs so workers can reach their individual potential and achieve real satisfaction.

We need to overcome organizational inertia and build ways to get workers involved in work planning, not merely with the suggestion box of the past but with new and vital employee idea contribution programs. We need to involve people not just for their labor input, but for their ideas and support. Workers who achieve a high level of satisfaction from their jobs develop a commitment to improvement. Organizations and workers alike benefit when the workers begin to think like change agents.

There are other significant reasons why employees should become change agents. The birth rate decline during the 1930s has affected the age profile of the American workforce. Today's worker ranks are being filled by younger, less experienced, but better educated workers. Because of limited work experience, their attitude about work is flexible, but is also demanding. They shun boring, repetitive work. Their education and flexibility are reflected in greater pressures for change. Like it or not, the young are becoming powerful change agents.

With their educational background and ability to adapt, the young make excellent, albeit inexperienced, agents for change. Properly directed, such a role can give them a challenging and rewarding outlet for their energies. It can also give them a means to accomplish change within a system organized for such purposes.

Anyone can be a change agent. It's not where you are in the organization but what you do that counts. Indeed, the lower your position and the greater your familiarity with the work, the easier it is to recognize what should be altered. The higher your position, the more grandiose your proposals for change, but many of them will be ill conceived because you lack a knowledge of detail.

Before we close our case for change agents, we have to look more closely at organizations and why they have become victims of change. In the next chapter and throughout the book we'll focus on change agents in business organizations. The reason for this is that business enterprises, because they operate in a competitive environment, have more highly developed mechanisms for accomplishing change than organizations operating in less competitive surroundings. But the rules of conduct, the need for meaningful change, and the need for change agents exist in all organizations, and the ideas herein can be adapted to fit the unique requirements of every organization.

THE ORGANIZATION: VICTIM OF CHANGE

Technological progress in the past decade has created so many new materials, processes, and manufacturing techniques that the possible combinations of products and the means of getting them stagger the imagination. Consumers can choose from a host of options in materials, quality, price, service features, dependability, style, color, and shape. Never before have they had such freedom of choice. But creating and satisfying product demands have put manufacturing organizations in an anomalous position as not only willing contributors to change, but also its unwilling victims. It is a perverse sort of logic, but if the corporation is to survive and succeed, it and all of its parts are forced to cope with change.

Change is not new; it is a normal part of life. What is new is the pace of change, now so rapid that most companies cannot respond properly. This has left them vulnerable to attack on two fronts: from people within the organization and from competition spurred by ever increasing technological capability.

The corporation is a victim of change because of this conflict. External forces demand change; internal forces press for it, while others favor the status quo. The host of external forces is impressive indeed. Customers seek improved products and services, and competition forces the corporation to provide them. The corporation is a victim of *moon logic;* it suffers from the "Why can't we?" syndrome. The corporate listening device for consumer preferences and attitudes is its market research, which studies and dutifully reports what the man on the street is thinking.

What the man on the street thinks is colored by moon logic, which goes like this: If we land men on the moon, why can't we make a can opener that doesn't jam or an appliance that doesn't break down? This logic isn't limited to products; it extends to medicine (Why can't we cure the common cold?) and government (Why can't we stop pollution and rebuild our decaying cities?). This "Why can't we?" moon logic is translated by the corporation into "We can." And so it does, in pursuit of profit.

Outside Forces for Change

Our rapidly changing world affects consumer buying habits, which in turn affect corporate marketing patterns. In its 1971 annual report to stockholders, Consolidated Foods Corporation viewed the impact of consumer preferences rather poetically:

> . . . the companies that make up Consolidated Foods Corporation are engaged in the production of a

myriad of goods and services that respond to the needs and desires of consumers.

We go about this task with respect for the fact that consumers quite properly have a freedom of choice and need not compromise their expectations. Consequently, they are loyal when satisfied and not forgetful when disappointed. By their decisions in the marketplace, they mold and shape the American economy and exert a pervasive influence on the fortunes of our Corporation.

Thus the corporation chases the illusive consumer, hoping to display its wares in such a way as to capture the public's fancy and dollars. In the face of shifting public moods, the corporation gropes for the proper combination of quality, service, brands, and image.

Although a powerful factor, the consumer isn't the only external force working on the corporation. Stockholders seek profits today and greater profits tomorrow, and the corporation has to change if it is to satisfy stockholders. The government impinges on corporate life by taxation, involvement in employee records, welfare, pollution control, product safety, and consumer welfare. Suppliers offer products and services in an ever widening array, which precipitate changes to incorporate these new offerings. Increasing complexities in business demand the use of outside service organizations such as consultants, auditors, lawyers, tax advisers, advertising agencies, and public relations firms. Moreover, the internal workings of the corporation must be geared to work with these outside agencies. The list of external forces can go on, but it is clear that the corporation is bombarded with the forces of increasingly complex changes.

How can the corporation respond to external pressures for change? The impact of the outside world on the corporation is too important to leave in the hands of novices; it requires knowledgeable change agents who can weigh the import of these external pressures and develop a coordinated strategy to meet changing world conditions.

The Internal Struggle

Let's turn now to an internal view of the corporation. Because some internal forces demand change while others resist it, all organizations are in tension and conflict. As the rate of change accelerates, these tensions and conflicts reach a point where useless friction and bickering consume the energies that should be devoted to productive purposes. Controlled tension and conflict can serve the best interests of the organization, but it takes change agents to provide this control.

To understand how change affects the inner workings of an organization, we can compare today's organization with the days when business was simple. There was a time when production would build a product and sales would sell it. Today, the arrangements are infinitely more complex. In addition to the regular production staff, every large manufacturing company has production control, inventory control, quality control, maintenance; process engineering, product engineering, industrial engineering, tool

27

engineering, purchasing, traffic, materials handling, and a host of other special departments.

At the selling end, in addition to salesmen, the large company has a management staff, advertising, sales promotion, customer service, contract administration, market research, statistics, sales planning and administration, and a host of others. Incoming orders are the province of order processing, billing, bookkeeping, accounting, banking and cash management, cost accounting and controls, credits and collections, financial planning, insurance, property control, taxes, systems and procedures, a computer, programmers, keypunchers, and a data processing manager. Finally, a personnel department does the hiring and sees to the fringe benefits to keep these people happy.

Specialization and Conflict

Because of the values derived from the specialization of labor, we live in an age dedicated to its perpetuation. More and more jobs that previously were all-encompassing have splintered into many subjobs, each requiring specialists with their own orientation and expertise. This proliferation of specialists has had its impact upon the corporation and how it manages change.

With all the change going on, corporations have to run just to keep up. But how can the average corporation keep up, given its limited resources and limited time? The proliferation of functional specialization is itself evidence of attempts to cope with change. Yet it serves to thwart change. Communication problems increase exponentially with the number of functions. And, significantly, each function has its own ax to grind. But outside pressures have forced organizations to become change oriented.

In response to internal and external stimuli some organizations have assigned change responsibility to each manager within his own area. For example, a marketing vice president is expected to develop and implement changes within his own department. This tactic leaves something to be desired because it makes no allowance for broad-gauged changes that affect more than one function. What if the marketing vice president wants to initiate a change that affects production? Who is responsible for such a move? Suppose a marketing vice president wanted to introduce a line of new products. Production would have to schedule the products, purchasing would have to buy the necessary parts, inventory control would have to maintain an inventory position on these parts, and the warehouse would have to stock and ship the products. Perhaps the marketing vice president's strategy would increase sales; perhaps it would insure the firm's survival. How would he accomplish this change?

The traditional approach has the managers of the affected departments decide what action and reactions are necessary. In this instance the marketing vice president would sit down with the managers of the other departments and discuss how to proceed. But translating marketing needs to a broader horizon is often difficult. Engineering cannot design and test new products unless it has additional manpower. Production cannot take on the added workload unless it has more plant capacity. The financial vice president has already limited purchases of inventory for existing products. And the warehouse is already full of existing products. But let us assume that each manager could, if he wanted to, take on his appointed task. Would the marketing vice president be likely to get the cooperation he needs? Unhappily, no. The other functions will cooperate only if cooperation would help them meet their *own* goals.

The sales vice president's goal is to sell the most items, which to him means having a wide variety of colors, styles, models, and options. Production's goal is quite different. This department would like to simplify its processes by having few items and little variety. Such limitations allow for production efficiency and reduced costs.

Engineering may want to design and test new products. But the inventory control people are already busy keeping track of parts for existing products, and new products would give them new headaches. Besides, the inventory control budget doesn't get any bigger because there are more parts to keep track of. And the people who run the warehouse don't want any more new products; it is already filled to overflowing, and new products wouldn't make their job any easier.

Thus whether a manager sees the push for new products as an opportunity or an additional headache depends on the impact of the change on his particular function. Those who find the proposal in conflict with their goals will be inclined to thwart the new product. Because this management decision has its roots in organizational conflict, a political struggle is inevitable in which there is a tendency to sidetrack change. Thus in the change-conflict cycle, suggested changes precipitate conflict which in turn serves to block change.

When a suggested change evokes conflict, some accommodation eventually has to be achieved between the parties. The most acceptable accommodation is to maintain the status quo since any change is looked upon as a movement away from normality. Both parties evaluate a proposal change in the same terms: Does it enhance our position? But the full implication of change can rarely be ascertained in advance. As a result, any stated reason for change is cause for suspicion. If the arguments are overwhelming, the proposal may stand a chance. But typically, great effort is required to convince enough important people. Since the root of this problem is conflict, a change agent is needed to act as conflict controller: keep in the forefront the interests of the total organization, and rise above departmental bias. Why not the president? He is too busy with his own tasks, which today's world has made infinitely more complex. The change agent serves as his delegate to control functional conflict and tension.

Many organizations seem unable to change simply because the change-conflict cycle has caught them on dead center. Sam Goodman, controller of the Nestlé Company, Inc., has done something about this. His extensive corporate and academic experience helped him identify three problems as typical in many corporations:

31

1. Accounting, finance, and marketing are insulated from one another.
2. Organization charts encourage inbreeding and isolation.
3. Individual, department, division, or company performance is too frequently measured by sales, not profits.

To overcome these problems he developed a marketing controller concept that integrates marketing and financial decision making, with the marketing controller acting as a change agent. By integrating marketing and finance Nestlé has been able to avoid much of the conflict that ordinarily occurs between these departments. Moreover, it has been able to improve marketing performance by giving marketing people the financial information they need for profitable decisions.

Nestlé's experience with marketing and finance points the way for other uses of change agents: to integrate production and finance, for example, or to integrate production and marketing. As a practical matter, change agents should be used to integrate departments where the greatest conflict exists. Marketing-oriented companies may find the solution in a marketing controller, as Nestlé did; other organizations may find it elsewhere.

The Change Quotient

A company's change quotient is its ability to change the things that require change. Some companies are true innovators; others are satisfied with carbon copies or variations of their competitors' products. Some companies change too much, and some change the wrong things. In some, change is limited to certain departments which are more responsive to change. Some companies have been able to balance change in all their departments; others have not.

Apparently, corporate change has largely been limited to technical and marketing innovation. Through technical innovation, companies have increased the quantity and quality of products and processes. Through marketing innovation they've increased their market penetration or opened new markets. But balanced change requires that all departments participate and that their efforts be coordinated, yet this is rarely the case, even in companies with a high change quotient.

For example, marketing may strive to be truly innovative in response to the company's markets, but the research and development function may be dragging its heels. Or R&D may be very aggressive but find an unresponsive marketing group frustrating its efforts. If, by some happy circumstance, R&D and marketing are in tune with each other, they still have to contend with the accountants. And the typical accountant is more concerned with custodial accounting than with the implications of change on corporate assets, even though impending changes could have a drastic effect on future profits. His carefully developed balance sheet reflects only yesterday's assets, which may already be obsolete, and it does not reflect the value of managerial talent, which is one of the greatest assets in changing times.

Organizational Senility and Decay

As organizations mature and management becomes entrenched, they tend to become rigid, even senile. John W. Gardner put it this way:

> When organizations and societies are young, they are flexible, fluid, not yet paralyzed by rigid specialization, and willing to try anything once. As the organization or society ages, vitality diminishes, flexibility gives way to rigidity, creativity fades and there is a loss of capacity to meet challenges from unexpected directions. Call to mind the adaptability of youth, and the way in which that adaptability diminished with the years. Call to mind the vigor and recklessness of some new organizations and societies—our own frontier settlements, for example—and reflect how frequently these qualities are buried under the weight of tradition and history.[1]

Evidence of organizational senility can be found in the low survival rate of ideas, which is minimal in aged and highly political structures. Trying out new ideas means taking chances, and each has a degree of risk associated with it. Senile organizations are so controlled that they don't take chances.

Working as a change agent, John W. Gardner has launched Common Cause, a citizen's lobby to press for change in social and political institutions. His reasons are enlightening: he sees (1) the widespread

[1] *Self-Renewal: The Individual and the Innovative Society* (New York: Harper & Row, 1964), p. 3.

failure of government at all levels to solve problems; (2) failure of performances in almost every area of the public process; (3) widespread institutional decay. Institutional reform, he contends, has been impeded by the absence of any pressure group (change agent) to make the case for such general reform to the public and to support public officials who try to enact it.

Mr. Gardner is attempting to tackle the problem of organization senility and decay on a national scale, but these symptoms exist to some degree in all mature institutions. In a freely competitive market, corporations are kept on their toes by the pricing policy of competitors. However, many markets are not freely competitive. Some are monopolistic; others are limited by technological as well as capital requirements. Some companies find that competitive pressures aren't enough to keep them on their toes; they need another means of making sure they don't become so habit-ridden that when a competitor does come along they can't survive. How can an organization fight internal decay? The change agent, using measured and timed stimulants, combats organizational senility and decay.

The Organization and Human Needs

Business firms are not run on a democratic basis; employees do not elect the company president, and they have no say in policy decisions. In fact, the modern corporation is more a dictatorship than a democracy. Admittedly, it is a benign dictatorship; its employees receive a great many benefits and are free to leave if they so desire. But, for the duration of their employment, a dictatorial society limits their activities and makes conformity mandatory. Within this society, as employees strive for self-fulfillment but are frustrated at every turn, pressures for change build within the organization. When there is no opportunity for self-expression and self-fulfillment, these pressures lead to passive antiorganization feelings or even overt actions. Or employees lose interest in their work environment and seek satisfaction elsewhere. Change agents know how to provide employees with an enriched job experience and at the same time help the organization to benefit from its vast talent reservoir. Change agents know how to do this because they are sensitive to human needs.

Recently there has been a spate of books on the subject of people in organizations. *Up the Organization, The Peter Principle,* several by C. Northcote Parkinson, and others have poked fun at the system. Most of them have much truth in their messages, and perhaps this is the reason for their popularity. But poking fun at our institutions and organizations is symptomatic of something deeper. Humor has always been a means of pointing out deficiencies in the human condition. What is the real message? It is a cry of frustration from people who see themselves as victims of these institutions.

The average person is victimized in a number of ways. First, as a consumer of goods and services he is frustrated by high prices and poor quality. Second, he is victimized by a highly productive technological society that promises him leisure but gives him pollution, inflation, and inner turmoil. Last, he is victimized as an employee who performs work and receives pay but derives little satisfaction. Instead, his days are filled with tedium, conflict, anxiety, company politics, and rigidity. Of all this, what he finds most intolerable is the lack of satisfaction that goes with a sense of achievement.

That man does not live by bread alone is at least as true today as it was when it was first observed. There was a time when a person had the satisfaction of seeing the fruits of his labor. In today's world his contribution is indistinguishable from that of others in the maze of products or services his employer offers. So he has to find satisfaction and solace in other elements of his job. Of the many sources of satisfaction, only one is money, and it ranks low on the list. Yet many jobs offer pay and little else.

The satisfaction of accomplishment is often denied to today's employee because the political structure of his company defends the status quo and makes meaningful change impossible. Because of specialization, his work is so narrow that it uses few of his talents and capabilities. Yet, bored though he may be, he often has no way out. He must work for a living, and that usually means working for someone else.

More than ever before, the typical worker in the United States is an employee of a medium-size or large corporation. In the days when we were a wilderness society, if a person didn't like his job or

surroundings he could easily move to another location, find a livelihood more to his liking, perhaps
even strike it rich in new ventures. Today, the capital
requirements to go into business are prohibitive for
most people. Hence the entrepreneurial opportunity
to enter the ranks of small business has been largely
diminished.

An inventor in bygone days needed little equipment or sophisticated gear. Because relatively little
was known, most of what he needed to know could be
kept in his head. Today the art of invention has for
the most part been relegated to the research and
development laboratories of industry where costly
equipment is available and computers keep up with
the state of the art. Modern merchandising techniques and volume price advantages are putting the
small merchant out of business. Costly inventory
commitments and expensive production facilities
limit manufacturing opportunities to companies
large enough to afford the financial investment. Although every day we see efforts to save endangered
species of wildlife, no one seems to care much
about the most endangered species of all—the
small businessman.

At one time, the small businessman was
considered the backbone of America, but this is no
longer the case. It's not only difficult to start a small
business; those already in existence are being gob-
bled up in mergers and acquisitions or have been
linked into bigger units for economic reasons. Big-
ness for its own sake has become the goal.

Well, what's wrong with working for somebody
else? Perhaps nothing. Many people consider such

an arrangement ideal. But others find themselves locked into highly structured jobs in highly structured environments that allow them no possibility of realizing their full potential. What is more, from coast to coast, jobs have been homogenized and standardized to the point where only the climate differs. The job of an aircraft structural engineer is substantially the same in New York, Texas, or California; and an accountant has to abide by the same basic principles and procedures no matter where he works.

In a typical organization an employee is confronted with rigidity and ineptitude and red tape that make it impossible for him to do things the way he would like to do them. He sees his job as stupid or irrelevant and his superiors as inept or compliant. And he is frustrated by the organization's inability to adapt itself to his human needs and the needs of his co-workers.

There was a time when established business institutions didn't have to withstand this barrage of criticism. Their contributions allowed us to achieve the standard of living which we would hardly elect to do without. But we have now moved into a new era, and many organizations are under attack because of their inability to keep pace with changing conditions and meet the human needs of employees for meaningful work and self-fulfillment.

The change agent can do something about making work meaningful. Job enrichment, job enlargement, job rotation, and work teams can turn dull, monotonous work into challenging and fulfilling tasks. He can tap the human potential that exists in every organization by motivating people to use their brain power creatively. The change agent is the bridge between human and organizational needs. People need fulfillment, and organizations need to cope with change. The two needs go hand in hand. The change agent provides the impetus to match and meet both needs.

II
HOW TO BE
A CHANGE AGENT

A MATTER OF SURVIVAL

It is an undisputed fact that the business death rate is high. Before each company became a cold statistic, it struggled to survive increased costs, competitive pressures, labor difficulties, and other problems. Each of these companies had well-intentioned people and a host of other resources at its command. Yet each managed to fail rather than succeed. Why do some businesses fail and others survive? Survival rests on the ability to change the right things at the right time; failure is the direct result of an inability to make an accurate self-diagnosis. The point can be illustrated with a fable concerning a company that had precisely this difficulty.

Once there was a company that employed the finest craftsmen who made the best product of its type obtainable anywhere. On each item the company sold, it made a small profit. The problem was that it didn't sell enough. As a result, business was not good.

The owner of the company called a meeting of his fine craftsmen and told them the problem. "We make a fine product but we don't sell enough of it to make much money. How can we make more money?"

The craftsmen gave the problem considerable thought and discussion before they agreed. "We're not selling enough because our raw material is so poor and so difficult to work that it causes imperfections in our product. Therefore, if we get better raw material we will sell more and make more money."

The owner respected the opinion of his craftsmen, who knew the product better than anybody, so he sought out and bought the best raw material in all the land. But, alas, the new raw material was so costly that, as time went on, instead of making more money the company made less.

Again the owner called in his craftsmen and told them the problem. They discussed it at length and finally agreed that the grinding wheels used to finish the product were too coarse. For a proper finish, which would give the product more sales appeal, grinding wheels with the smoothest possible texture must be secured. So the owner searched for a new supplier of grinding wheels. After considerable effort in locating and installing the new grinding wheels, a finished product was turned out that was far superior to the old, but it did not improve sales enough to justify the cost of the new, smooth-textured grinding wheels.

The company now made less money than ever before. And the owner called in his craftsmen and explained the problem. This time the craftsmen argued all night, but finally they agreed that the real problem was the factory itself. Some craftsmen needed more light, others needed more tools, and still others needed more space.

A list was made of all the problems, and the owner hired work crews to make alterations so the craftsmen could work under the best possible conditions. Alas, between the work stoppage for factory repairs and the cost of the repairs themselves, there was no profit. Indeed, before the repairs were finished the money ran out and the factory closed its doors.

This simple example gives us an interesting lesson in survival. Had this company's owner recognized what was happening, when it was happening, he might have corrected the mistakes before it was too late. But he was so close to the problem and so enmeshed in details that his overall vision was clouded and he overlooked the real problem, sales, as well as the opportunities that could have brought success.

Often, businessmen look in only one or two directions for answers to problems that call for a multidirectional problem-solving approach. Often, too, they listen to people who give them limited answers when they should seek out and listen to those who offer a wider variety of alternatives. Most important, they avoid the role of true change agent because they lack the time and skill to perform as a change agent would. Many a businessman is so busy doing the things he likes to do that he has no time for the things he should do. Calling on the trade when internal difficulties need to be straightened away is a direct route to oblivion. When the pace of change was not so quick, when markets, production processes, and product technology were relatively stable, a business could count on grinding out and selling the same old products for years on end. But today's rate of change demands responsiveness. It demands that businessmen function as change agents.

Changing a businessman's work habits is not easy. And functioning as a change agent is hard work—perhaps the hardest work he will ever do. But the management of a business has never been easy, and today, if anything, the job is infinitely more complex.

The craftsmen fable is a valuable lesson in the kinds of mistakes that all businesses make to some degree. These blunders may not be enough to destroy a business on the spot, since each blunder may only reduce profits a little bit. But if enough of these profit leaks go unchecked for any length of time, the profits—the lifeblood of a business—will drain away and the company itself will die. To gain further insight into the problems of self-diagnosis, let's consider some of the things that companies do to speed their own demise.

When a company is not doing well its executives may refuse to admit it and may put forth impressive arguments to justify their poor showing. A clever executive may even make it appear that he alone can turn the tide of events and may convince everyone, including himself, that if it weren't for him, things would be much worse.

Dodging the truth can go on for some time. Consider the Penn-Central Railroad, whose complex accounting information was digested, consolidated, and disguised to such an extent that even sophisticated investors couldn't determine the seriousness of the company's financial crisis. Such delaying tactics forestall any attempt to face the facts. The complexity of business makes it all the more difficult to pin down the depth and breadth of such problems, and business is getting more complex all the time.

45

Distinguishing Problems from Symptoms

Eventually, a company that is sliding downhill has to admit to the seriousness of the situation. The time is then at hand when the leaders begin seeking answers to their problems and can no longer be satisfied with excuses. This is the critical time. For what they do and how they do it will determine whether they survive.

Before a company can get well it has to recognize the nature and magnitude of its illness. Often companies confuse symptoms for problems and then treat the symptoms. This serves to ignore the real trouble and slow the recovery process. It also deludes managers into thinking they're doing all they can and things are bound to get better soon. For example, cumbersome procedures, excessive paperwork, and many authorized signatures are often cited as typical problems in bureaucratic organizations. But these forms of red tape are merely the manifestations of deep-seated problems such as poor communication, personal insecurity, or inept management. Red tape isn't a problem; it's a symptom. Cutting red tape will solve nothing; it will merely grow back again unless the problems it represents can be solved.

Before the decision makers can treat a sick company they must identify the problem. Just what factor or combination of factors is causing the problem? How deep is the wound? Will emergency first aid be enough? Can the company itself apply the first aid or should it seek outside help? Contrary to popular belief, diagnosis of business problems is not a simple matter. The distinction between symptoms and problems is often subtle, but a change agent is an expert in detecting such subtleties.

Consider what happened to one company that did not have a knowledgeable change agent. Management perceived its problem to be too many people. Because labor costs were too high, it cut back on low-level personnel. But, as time went by, labor costs climbed. A year later the company began the same campaign again, and again labor costs climbed as people were added to the payroll. This seesaw state of affairs went on for a number of years.

On the surface the company appeared to be grappling with the real problem: to control costs. In truth, the high labor costs were symptomatic of a more basic problem—that of poor management. Stubbornly refusing to seek better work methods, management had let work procedures get hopelessly out of date, and it was the company's inefficient methods that necessitated too much labor in the first place. Because what appeared to be a labor cost problem was in reality a management problem, no amount of effort directed to labor costs alone could cure the company's ailment.

The business owner in our fable didn't tackle his real problem either. True, he asked for help. But he addressed himself to craftsmen and they answered in the only way they could: by telling him how to create a better product. Since the problem was sales, not product improvement, a change agent would have sought answers in the marketplace. In short order, customers and potential customers would have told him what he needed to know. Then the company could have responded by giving customers what they really wanted rather than what the craftsmen thought they wanted.

Changing the Wrong Things

It is obvious to even the most unsophisticated that survival in a rapidly changing world demands change. Yet change is easier to talk about than to accomplish. Why did the companies we discussed change the wrong things? Because change can be traumatic, many companies make easy changes rather than necessary ones, on the assumption that doing something is better than doing nothing at all. The company that annually cut its labor costs did so because it was far easier to do this than to alter policy. And the owner of the business that failed consulted his craftsmen because it was easy to do and subconsciously he was afraid to learn what his customers might say about his product. The results were predictable, but he pursued his warped logic to the end, steadfast in his belief that more and more quality would eventually pay off.

So, too, many companies change the wrong things because they are psychologically unable to change the things they should. This inability to change afflicts all executives to some degree. Change requires a great deal of mental flexibility, particularly if it is broad in scope. Many executives are ill-equipped to make sweeping changes because their years of business experience have locked them into certain work response patterns. So they adjust peripheral details and leave the fundamental problems unresolved. Since these executives collectively are the company, it's no wonder that so many companies are changing the wrong things.

Work habits can keep anyone in a rut that may be comfortable and even successful. The danger lies in the fact that a rut limits experience, exposure, pressure, and opportunity. Advancement comes only to those willing and able to move beyond what they are now doing and widen their horizons. Yet widening one's horizon can be a frustrating, harrowing, and even dangerous experience.

An eminently successful salesman owed his success to certain well-developed sales habits which were ingrained into his work personality. As a reward for his success he was made sales manager. But he could never quite make the transition because he could never stop selling long enough to learn how to manage. For the company it was an obvious case of losing a good salesman and gaining a poor manager. Why did this salesman fail? He was so well conditioned to selling that he couldn't stop. For him, selling was a conditioned response, an automatic reflex that occurred involuntarily and one he couldn't control.

The Selling President

An example of the inability to change occurred in a company that elevated a sales vice president to the post of company president as a reward for outstanding success in sales. The new president was in reality a glorified salesman whose success was largely due to his ability to get along well with key house accounts and maintain a steady volume of sales to them. But he knew little about the other aspects of the business such as finance, accounting, production and inventory control, shipping, and engineering.

When he assumed the duties of president, he made some attempts to broaden his knowledge of the company. But he was under pressure to make a showing as a successful president, and it was easier to do the things he knew and liked best, so he concentrated on selling and in short order became a part-time selling president.

Because of his heavy involvement in selling, he delegated the responsibilities for finance, engineering, and production to others. But major decisions had to wait until he returned from a sales trip. In this managerial vacuum without adequate leadership, the factory and home office became a battleground in a power struggle between his vice presidents. During this period costs began to climb alarmingly.

Up until this time the president spent a portion of his time in the office, but his efforts even then were confined to marketing decisions. Faced with increasing costs and dwindling profits, he reverted even more to his earlier work habits and decided to concentrate on personal selling. Now he was almost totally unavailable for his true role as president. Things got worse before they got better, and they got better only when the selling president was finally replaced.

Companies, like individuals, demonstrate this same inability to change. Some have produced goods long after the market for them disappeared. But consumer demand patterns shift, and product life cycles get shorter. New products from competitors make obsolete existing stocks of merchandise. To keep pace, a company has to develop a market intelligence network and the internal mechanisms to respond to changing preferences.

Companies also get locked into certain response patterns. Some sales-oriented companies are so dominated by sales thinking that their efforts are devoted solely in that direction to the detriment of other elements of the company. One such company doggedly pursued sales when its factory was hopelessly obsolete. If it had modernized production it could have reduced selling prices (which would increase sales potential) and at the same time increased profits substantially . As it was, the more the company sold, the less money it made.

Production-oriented companies are no better. They think more profits come from producing goods a little cheaper or a little faster. They suffer from the same kind of nearsightedness and neglect the sales side of their business. Once a company begins moving in a certain direction, an inertia effect builds up which causes it to move in that direction even faster. Thus when profits are derived largely from technological skills, management strongly supports enlargement of those skills and tends to downgrade other efforts. Companies need change agents who can rise above the emotional issues; face facts, no matter how brutal they may be; and make the right changes, no matter how difficult—because they know that in the long run survival depends on these changes.

Managing Innovation

Change characterizes our lives; to control and direct it, we have to plan for it. Planned change has been defined as "a conscious, deliberate, and collaborative effort to improve the operations of a system, whether it be a self-system, social system, or cultural system, through the utilization of scientific knowledge."[1]

Organizations with depth of experience in managing change have found that the *way* in which change is managed is critical and that there has to be an organized, deliberate, planned approach. Assigning change responsibility to an already overburdened manager is not the answer. Mechanisms to accomplish change must be developed, and a positive orientation toward change must be inoculated into the organizational bloodstream. When a positive change climate is established it will enhance the effectiveness of all change agents.

In some companies, change is considered synonymous with innovation; other companies associate innovation only with research and development. But innovation can occur in production and marketing as well. In fact, effective management of innovation results from an integration of all three categories: research and development, production, and marketing. A company that is outstanding in research and development but weak in production and marketing innovation will be outperformed by another organi-

---

[1] Warren G. Bennis, K. D. Benne, and R. Chin, eds., *The Planning of Change: Readings in the Applied Behavioral Sciences* (New York: Holt, Rinehart and Winston, 1961), Chapter 2.

zation with a better balance of innovation in all three categories.

Production innovation was dramatically illustrated by the first use of mass and mechanized assembly methods at the Ford Motor Company. The concept of the moving assembly line spread through Ford in 1914 and 1915 from one magneto line chassis assembly and then to the assembly of body and chassis. Indeed, continuous movement through assembly operations is one of the milestones in manufacturing history. This innovation brought about mass marketing of automobiles and the creation of the automobile industry as we know it today.

This production innovation in turn triggered a marketing innovation. With the high-volume, low-priced, single-style Model-T, the Ford Motor Company captured more than 50 percent of the automobile market in 1921. In that same year General Motors Corporation developed a radically different marketing innovation: regular upgrading of the product and recognition of the growing desire for a variety of models to meet the needs of buyers across a broad price spectrum.

Yet another fundamental marketing innovation was the brainchild of a young United States army officer stationed in Panama, late in the nineteenth century. There he read statistical abstracts concerning per capita incomes of farm families in the United States. Putting this together with previously read statistical information on expansion of the postal system in the United States, he evolved the concept of selling to rural areas by mail. The entire mail-order industry as we know it today developed from this

humble beginning. The name of the company—
Sears, Roebuck.

Texas Instruments Incorporated is a Dallas firm
heavily engaged in technological change and research and development programs. Not content with
its innovative capability in research and development, it has evolved concepts for innovation responsibility in production and marketing as well. To do
this, the company details its various business objectives, then decides on strategies and tactics which
allow it to meet these objectives.

Texas Instruments' success in semiconductors
was the result of an R&D breakthrough. Establish-
ment of a materials-oriented research laboratory, introduction of the first silicon transistor and the first
all-transistor pocket radio, and the development of a
process for making pure silicon were all successful
tactics that helped Texas Instruments seize the lead
in the semiconductor industry from larger companies.

It was after this series of successes that Texas
Instruments' top executives began to recognize the
success pattern of well-conceived strategies and
well-carried-out supporting tactics. And it was then
that they detached one of their senior officers from
other duties to devote all his time to the study and
implementation of a formal system for accomplishing innovative successes. Acting as top-level change
agent, the executive initiated a system to identify the
strategies that should be followed for growth and
development. At the same time he also identified the
individual change agents who would implement the
strategies. By this means, he succeeded in diffusing

the change agent concept and the responsibility for initiating innovative programs throughout the company.

Innovation can create industries and improve profits. But innovation doesn't happen automatically; it takes change agents who can pave the way. For example, a small electronics company with a wide variety of products had difficulty in production operations whenever there was a change in the product line. Since the product line was changed frequently, it was necessary to develop new methods of gearing to this change. The firm's change agent was influential in having mobile work benches designed with the proper parts for the specific product assembly. Teams of individual workers were designated. When the time came to make a production change, the production teams were assigned and the proper benches rolled out into place. Production proceeded within a matter of hours rather than days.

In another case a change agent in a warehousing operation with a highly seasonal business had the seasonal items put on mobile racks which were moved close to the nerve center of the warehouse at the height of the season. The racks were kept in a storage area during the slow season, with items stored on each rack rather than shifted from one rack to another. This innovation saved considerable time and money.

In many organizations change through innovation is a way of life. Profit-motivated companies exist to create, make, and market useful products and services that satisfy the needs of customers in order to make a profit. If companies are to prosper, to grow, to broaden, and to improve the products and services they offer, they must be so managed as to insure a high level of long-term profitability. Corporate survival begins with innovation, and change agents manage that innovation.

Companies with competitive advantages such as patent protection, unique technological capability, or costly manufacturing facilities may dismiss innovation as something for the future. But less protected companies are experiencing increased competitive pressures, and technological changes in materials and production processes are dramatically affecting others. For these companies, innovation responsibility makes a lot of sense.

Even protected organizations would do well to begin planning for innovation responsibility, using change agents as catalysts of change. One never knows when seemingly impregnable protection will dissolve. Indeed, a future barometer of corporate health may well be the rating on an innovation scale rather than the traditional balance sheet and profit and loss statement. Even nonprofit institutions and government agencies have the specter of rapid social change hanging over their heads. They, too, need change agents to make their organizations alert and responsive to the needs of the people they serve.

Organizational survival in the future will depend on change agents capable of recognizing and treating problems, not symptoms, and of changing the right things. All organizations will have to learn to manage change the way Texas Instruments learned to manage innovation. The only question is how quickly they will have to do this. Companies in the forefront of technological innovation as well as those that have been highly responsive to change in their environment have found the secret to survival, and their ideas can be adapted in varying degrees to all organizations.

PRACTICING THE ART OF CHANGE

Organizations are made up of people working in concert toward some common goal. It is people who create a viable organization and breathe life and purpose into its structure. It is people with their strengths and weaknesses who give the organization color and depth. Their creativeness, skill, individuality, and drive contribute to its strength. But these qualities can dimish as well as enhance an organization's ability to change. No change that depends on people can ever be completely predict..Jle because people are never completely predictable. The human organism is a complex blend of preconditioned psychological attitudes based on a variety of educational, personal, and work experiences. Each person bases his decisions on these experiences. Each brings to his work prejudice, predilection, and a unique personality. To a degree, each personality requires special handling. Any movement or change from what is considered normal has to take into account these personalities if it is to be successful.

By comparison, changing a completely automated factory is a simple procedure. Since no unique personalities are involved, it becomes a matter of making a plan and then implementing it. Without people, change is a cold, sterile, predictable business; with people, it is an art as opposed to a science.

The change agent is a practitioner of the art of change. He knows that scientific management tools and concepts work beautifully if applied to the right business problem at the right time. He also knows change techniques and that melding techniques into the fabric or climate of the organization is where problems arise. Knowing when and what to use and where it applies is part of the art of change. It is in the proper practice of this art that change agents are worth their weight in gold. They may use management sciences to help in their practice—but they don't confuse science and practice.

The Business Doctor

In many ways the change agent's job is much like the family doctor's job. When you become ill you try your favorite home remedies: aspirin, a hot water bottle, a good night's sleep. You have made a self-diagnosis of your ills and implemented corrective action. If the home remedies work, nothing more is needed. If they do not work, you take the next step: a visit to your doctor, who uses scientific techniques, asks for your symptoms, and calls upon his experience with similar situations to find out what's wrong with you.

The scientific tests—blood pressure, temperature, electrocardiogram, and so on—tell him the magnitude of the problem as well as help support his diagnosis. In categorizing your symptoms and tests, he relies on the body of knowledge in medical textbooks and journals as well as his experience over the time he has been in practice.

Given the diagnosis and the prescription that generally follows, you go to your local pharmacy and receive a supply of pills which your doctor has prescribed to cure your illness. Now, if the pills do the job and you get better, your estimation of the doctor rises. However, if the pills do not work you may go back to your doctor, try other home remedies, or look for a different doctor. If you go back to the same doctor, he may reexamine you, repeat his diagnostic procedure, and prescribe other pills. This process is repeated until the disease wears itself out or wears you out, or until the doctor hits upon a treatment that makes you well. Now, what happened here? The doctor has been practicing medicine, and he has been practicing on you.

When illness strikes a company the manifestations may be dwindling profits, frequent customer complaints, bottlenecks, or a general uneasiness that something isn't going quite right. And just as in the case of personal illness, the reaction is to apply home remedies.

Self-diagnosis and treatment of business illness are automatic. The first logical step is a relatively objective evaluation of how sick the patient company really is. Until we know the magnitude and the nature of the illness, a stop-gap remedy may be the first solution. If we stumble upon something that seems to work, the firm survives to go on to the next ordeal.

There are times when a corporate aspirin is not enough, so we try other things. Often we grope for a remedy without really learning the cause of the illness. The symptoms may confuse us. For example, is it the kind of business problem that requires simply emergency first aid or is it more serious?

Problems are rarely clear enough to be acted upon when they are first discovered. The surface manifestations are at best symptoms, and often the least revealing ones. There is no shortcut to good problem definition. If it is to be effective it must be directed toward the underlying problem rather than a superficial symptom. For example, management may see excessive paperwork as a disease when actually it is symptomatic of an insecure organization. The real problem may be a loss of communication or control. It takes a change agent to find the real problems in short order because it is his job to do so. Without him, a company can get bogged down in lengthy unproductive efforts with little to show for them.

Testing for Business Ailments

Symptoms are readily observed, but diagnosis of corporate ailments takes real know-how. Here are some simple tests that help change agents determine whether a company is healthy enough to survive in a competitive environment.

The purchasing test. At the next convenient opportunity, wander down to the purchasing department and count the number of copies in a purchase order set. Find out whether a purchase requisition precedes the purchase order. Total the number of pieces of paper to initiate and complete a purchase transaction. Be sure to include the copies made and distributed on receipt of the purchased item. If the number of pieces of paper exceeds seven you may be in trouble.

Next find out how many purchase orders were written last year. Count the number of people in the purchasing department and divide this number into the number of purchase orders written. If the resultant figure is less than 50 you're in trouble.

The security test. Quietly advise the president of your company that you're going to steal something of value so as to test company security. Select a high-value, commonly available item that is not supposed to be taken off the premises. (A typewriter is a good test item.) Disguise it only slightly and try to get it out through the front door. If no one asks about it at the time, the company may be in trouble. If no one misses it after one week, you know there's trouble. Don't forget to return the item!

The telephone visit. On some pretext visit your accounting department and count the number of telephones. Then find out which employees have a legitimate need for a phone. (Phone calls home to find out what's for dinner don't count.) If you have more than one phone for each six employees you may be in trouble. If each desk has a phone, even though the employees don't conduct business on the phone, you know you're in trouble.

Tests like these apply to most businesses, and even a novice change agent can apply them. The diagnosis may call for emergency first aid. But if the trouble is more serious, emergency treatment won't necessarily make matters better. To go back to our medical analogy, if blood is flowing from a wound too rapidly, a tourniquet is sometimes appropriate first aid. But applying a tourniquet to the neck is no way to cure a head wound.

If preliminary tests indicate that your organization is sick, the next step is to be sure that the illness hasn't gone too far. To do so, check your organization's heartbeat by unobtrusively listening to the conversations of employees in the cafeteria or whenever they gather. Do employees accept conditions as they exist? This is the first sign of business paralysis, though not necessarily fatal. It results in a general lackadaisical attitude, customer complaints, an unresponsive organization, and, finally, profit reduction.

Next, observe the work pace in the factory. A sluggish pace is another symptom of business paralysis. Slow-moving companies assume that a slow pace is proof that quality is being built into the products. In most instances, however, just the reverse is true; a slow pace means less, not more, quality in a product.

Now observe the work pace in the office and compare it to what you observed in the factory. If the pace is faster in the office than in the factory, something is suspicious.

Next, compare the work pace in both factory and

office to the pace at the checkout counters of the supermarket in your neighborhood on a busy Saturday. If your company's pace is even close to that, you have nothing to worry about. If it's less than half that pace, further tests are in order.

Finally, check the organizational bloodstream. Do people appear listless or lackadaisical? Is the company loaded with underachievers; if so, why? Underachievers may have an easy job but they're not happy. They derive no satisfaction in their jobs and find outside outlets for their energies and talents.

To find where people spend their energies, drop in at the next regularly scheduled company athletic event to determine the attitude of the participants. Are they indulging in company golf or bowling at the expense of their jobs? Has the company bowling team become more important to them than the job itself?

A key barometer of company health is employee attitudes about profit, and the astute change agent can learn about these attitudes without official survey questionnaires, which employees tend to answer the way they think you want them answered. Playing detective by asking the right questions and keeping one's ears and eyes open pays big information dividends.

Curing a Sick Organization

Once the magnitude of a company's illness is known, carefully planned treatment by the change agent can begin. Just as a doctor practices medicine on his patients, a change agent, within the framework of his authority, practices change on his company. His diagnostic techniques may include statistical analysis, operations research, ratio analysis, financial analysis, and a host of other impressive and sophisticated analytical tools.

Sometimes it's difficult to determine which specific technique to use on the problems at hand. In the last analysis, the recommendations for treatment of the particular business illness are based largely on the change agent's intuitive judgment and skill. These, in turn, draw on all the facts that can be gathered together and all the scientific and analytical tools that can be applied to the problem. This is not an easy task. Anyone working within an organization is bound to lose some degree of objectivity. But the change agent's contribution can be significant if he can take a dispassionate view that gives him a perspective on what he has to do and how he has to do it.

A change agent's remedy for a sick organization may be reorganization and a realignment of departments and department heads. Or, if the environment in which the organization is operating has changed significantly and new marketing techniques are warranted, the change agent may realign the marketing channels and select new techniques for marketing the company's products.

Change agents have been known to replace existing department heads, make personnel changes up and down the organization, have new plants built in place of obsolete, old ones, try new layouts in existing

plants, or develop new procedures for internal handling of paperwork. All these techniques are clear
evidence of a change agent in search of solutions. But
the practice of change and problem solving is at best
an imprecise business that calls for diligence, hard
work, and sometimes sheer luck. Frequently, it is
unknown if a problem is solved until sometime after
action has been taken. Sometimes problems appear
to be solved, but in reality they have shifted into other
problems. That is, through hard work, the company
has traded one set of problems for another. Some
change agents liken their organizations to a piece of
putty. Pushing the putty to make it fit a mold at one
point may make it bulge elsewhere.

In medicine the ultimate test of a diagnosis and
treatment is whether the patient lives and returns to
normal. In the corporation profit or loss measures
the success of change agents. Yet profit is not necessarily proof that he is practicing his art properly.

Just as in human beings there are degrees or
gradations of normality, in a corporation there are
degrees or gradations of profit. To be earning a
profit may not be enough. The goal of the change
agent is to achieve the optimum profit with the resources available. How much more profit could have
been generated if a different approach to the problems had been taken? How much profit will be lost
because of ill-planned or ill-conceived sales campaigns? How much profit will be lost for lack of
planning in the areas of organization, products,
markets, and plant facilities?

The following chapters look at what change agents do to change the organization, people's at-titudes, and the work people do. Each is an attempt to combine the resources of men, money, and machines in such a way that the organization's total goals are achieved. But change agents know that the needs of the organization are best met when human needs are taken into account.

III

CHANGING
THE ORGANIZATION

THE FACTS OF BUSINESS LIFE

The production departments of a medium-size metalworking company were in turmoil whenever the president returned from a sales goodwill tour because his return always meant days of adjusting production schedules, juggling jobs, altering special machining setups, and interrupting production runs. To the foremen such indiscriminate schedule changes were idiotic as well as chaotic, and they voiced their complaints up the line to the production manager.

The production manager had been through this before and knew the futility of arguments. Be thankful the boss doesn't take these trips more often, he told his men. What he was saying was that this condition was a fact of business life. One of the more astute foremen summarized it to his men this way: "The sales tail here wags the production dog."

Certainly any supervisor who wants to get along has to adjust to the facts of life. In any sales-oriented company, one such fact is that production people have to accept rush orders and schedule changes even though everybody knows that rush orders upset existing production schedules, cause production downtime, waste materials, and generally reduce plant efficiency.

The production manager may rationalize that these interruptions are necessary, but he may not recognize that the conflict between departments is

68

natural and normal in any business operation. More important, management may not know what it is losing by such antics. Everyone knows that missed deadlines mean the loss of business. But what costs are incurred in *meeting* deadlines, and are these costs a fact of business life? Companies that operate in this way desperately need change agents who can interpret the facts and balance the profit contribution of each function within the company.

Most fledgling management men expect a business to run smoothly, be well coordinated, and have a minimum of internal friction or conflict. But growing, dynamic businesses do not run smoothly. In every healthy business, conflict exists. Moreover, it exists between certain organizational elements regardless of the nature of the business. For example, the man responsible for sales would like to sell everything to anybody, whereas the man responsible for credit would like to permit sales only to customers with top credit ratings. This is a natural conflict because the sales people are charged with the responsibility of selling the most products at the best price, whereas the credit people have the responsibility for determining whether the customer can pay for the merchandise.

Another natural conflict exists between the man responsible for sales and the man responsible for production. For example, sales might like to have the product in a wide variety of colors, styles, and models, whereas production would like to have as little variety as possible. This conflict is easy to understand when we remember that variety would increase sales but reduce production efficiency. A second natural conflict between sales and production lies in delivery schedules because sales people would like to have every order filled instantly, whereas the production people have to fit each new order into existing schedules. Yet other natural conflicts arise between quality control and production, between engineering and sales, and between engineering and production in every organization.

Conflict exists not only because of different goals but also because of the tendency to think one's own function is the most important because its contribution is the greatest. For example, an aircraft company's armament group is likely to visualize an airplane in terms of guns and bullets and bombs, but the electrical group's visualization centers on wires and switches and fuses and other electrical gadgetry. In other words, each group has its own orientation, its own frame of reference, and each sees its contribution to the total product as the most significant. Contribution distortion is commonplace. Some people are objective enough to recognize and admit to their bias once the big picture is clearly presented. Unhappily, most people are so enmeshed in their day-to-day duties that they never raise their sights beyond their immediate group's view. And often there is no one around to show them the big picture. The concept of management by objectives has come into vogue because it helps clear away this functional orientation fog.

Functional Polarization

Every company exhibits evidence of functional orientation and bias. Rarely, for example, do sales-

70

men or sales managers have kind things to say about the production team, and production people and their managers rarely have kind things to say about their sales force. Each group believes that without its contribution the company would have been out of business long ago, and each is convinced that if it weren't for the ridiculous demands of those other groups, the company would be far better off.

Robert Ardrey identifies many species of mammals that stake out an area of land that can support their food requirements. This territory is set aside by various means. The hippopotamus defecates and the wolf urinates on the territory's outer perimeter. These markings identify the boundary just as fences mark human territorial boundaries. The leader of the group, usually the dominant male, protects the territory from others of the same species and fights off interlopers. According to Ardrey, men living in nations operate by the same animal instinct to protect their territories in time of danger.[1]

The territorial imperative also covers people in organizations. Antony Jay points out that companies fighting for sales treat their share of the market as their own territory and that any attempt at encroachment is considered tantamount to a territorial invasion.[2] This marketing territorial imperative is an extension of Ardrey's thinking on an intercompany level. But territorial imperative doesn't stop there; it extends to the intracompany level where groups protect what they consider to be their domain.

---

[1] *The Territorial Imperative* (New York: Atheneum, 1966).
[2] *Management and Machiavelli* (New York: Holt, Rinehart and Winston, 1967) p. 32.

71

One link that binds people together is a professional or quasi-professional orientation. As Toffler put it: "The old loyalty felt by the organization men appears to be going up in smoke. In its place we are watching the rise of professional loyalty."[3]

In most businesses, professionals are grouped within functions for work control and organizational simplicity. Tables of organization or organization charts show these functions as neat little boxes representing engineering, accounting, sales, and so on. (The more rapidly changing industries have adapted their organization structures to project teams that intermix disciplines, but most people still work in the classic functional arrangements.) This separation by function creates a sense of territory which has to be protected from outsiders. Professional loyalty is easily translated into functional loyalty, and the professionals look inward to their own kind for understanding, strength, and solace in the face of external pressures.

Each function has a leader, its manager or supervisor, who provides a degree of order and tranquility. Surrounding each function are others seeking power and dominance. The functional leader will fight those functions encroaching on what the group considers its domain. Thus modern organizational squabbles and interdepartmental conflicts are merely manifestations of territorial instincts. It is as if each function were a separate tribe and the tribes were continually feuding; open warfare is rare but there are frequent border clashes. Even though all functions are part of the same organization, the pull

[3] *Future Shock* (New York: Random House, 1970), p. 131.

of the group is stronger. Yet in the last analysis it is the total organization that must flourish if each person in each group is to prosper.

By and large, companies bring this pox upon themselves by building organizations so rigid that they cannot make flexible use of flexible people. The fact is that, given some orientation and training, sales managers can become excellent production managers and production managers can expand their horizons tremendously by calling on customers. Yet few companies are willing to experiment with job rotation.

The Drive for Power

It might help if departments in companies could stand back and take an objective view of their contributions and their biases. But, alas, it's difficult to represent R&D, market research, order processing, and other assorted departments in a visual presentation of a typical company's products. Rarely are the employees of a large corporation made to feel part of the total team effort. Few are willing to subordinate their needs and the needs of their group to the needs of the corporation because few consider themselves part of the company.

In any organization, both people and functions aspire to power. The reasons for this power drive are spelled out by Antony Jay in this way:

> Most people who aspire to power within organizations will tell you that they want it so as to achieve objects they believe in, but even that does not go to the heart

of the matter. The real pleasure of power is the pleasure of freedom, and it goes right back to one of man's most primitive needs, the need to control his environment. You get no great sense of freedom if you are liable at any time to starve or freeze or be devoured by wolves or speared by a neighboring tribe, and so you set about securing a supply of food, shelter, warmth, and defensive weapons. Gradually you increase the control, and one of the most important ways you increase it is by organization, by making your tribe the biggest and strongest of the area, and of course by doing so you submit yourself to the control of environment again—the environment now being the organization you belong to—a much more agreeable one than before, but still outside your control. However, if you become a respected and successful person within the organization, you may begin to be involved in the control of it. You taste what some people call power, but to you it tastes of freedom. Your life is still partly regulated by the actions and decisions of others, but now a part of it is regulated according to your own choice and by your own decisions.[4]

Thus, individuals or, for that matter, entire departments see managerial control as an infringement on their freedom. They also reasonably believe that their view of the world is the most important, the most understanding, and the most profit-generating view for the corporation. Like the various groups manufacturing an airplane, individual departments view their function as the most important and believe it should therefore be subject to the least control.

However, if management were to give way to

[4] Op. cit., p. 38.

functional demands it would soon face the problems encountered by Frank Pace of General Dynamics. When he took over in 1957 he found himself virtually a prisoner of his own managers. His head office staff numbered 200 in a company of 106,000 made up of nine virtually autonomous divisions. Most of them had been independent enterprises before they joined and had their own separate legal and financial staffs as well as their own tough presidents. Pace decided to leave them more or less alone. The only way to success he said "is to operate on a decentralized basis." General Dynamics lost $425 million between 1960 and 1962, a sizable loss in anyone's book.

Who, then, can resolve conflict between functions and balance total corporate needs? Traditional thinking has it that if the parties can't agree let them go to the next organizational level for the decision. This can mean the president, but often he is the least qualified to resolve the conflict. Indeed, it was the president of the metalworking firm mentioned earlier who altered all production schedules whenever he returned from a sales goodwill tour. Presidents are often too busy with other matters to concern themselves with jurisdictional disputes. Then, too, the mere act of bringing a problem to the president's attention is an admission of failure.

How to Balance Conflict

If there is no real balancing force for natural conflict it will tend to take certain directions. For example, if the president of a company is sales oriented, sales will tend to dominate decisions. If, on the other hand, the president or decision maker is production oriented, the organization and decisions made will tend to favor production.When this happens, conflict may cease to exist but the business will be in mortal danger.

Sales without due regard to production needs or production without due regard to sales requirements will not do; there has to be a balancing process. This is where the change agent comes in. He keeps in mind that the goal of the organization is to generate profit over the long term and that each decision has to be based on the needs of the organization in the light of the capability of its people and facilities.

To eliminate natural conflict by becoming production or sales oriented is to eliminate one of the best forms of profit insurance. Just as the federal government maintains checks and balances through its executive, legislative, and judicial branches, so too any business must maintain checks and balances to avoid the use of uncontrolled power. True, the balancing required to keep an organization moving the right direction is difficult, time-consuming work. But it is a high order of the practice of management.

Balancing production and marketing needs is a particularly difficult task, since the two goals are at opposite extremes. Production schedules, like so many other business plans, are a series of compromises. These compromises are normally a balance between customer need and resource or capacity availability. The production manager accepts the need for balance but he also recognizes the need for

76

production efficiency. Paradoxically, as an organization's technical and productive capability increases, marketing becomes a more dominant factor in this balance.

Thus the production manager's life grows increasingly complex. When Henry Ford decided to sell cars in any color as long as it was black, it was the production manager in him that made the decision. Nowadays the public demands variety so the production manager has to live with varieties of styles, shapes, colors, and specifications that create a production nightmare. The nightmare becomes manageable by adding staff to keep track of the production web, which adds significantly to cost. Sometimes the added costs outweigh the added sales and sometimes profit considerations are overlooked in the push to keep up with the competition or round out the product line or expand the productive base. How simple production-life once was. How much more complex will it be tomorrow?

Because today we live in a marketing-oriented society, rash marketing decisions may be inadvertently rubber-stamped by top management. A manager who meekly accepts such decisions creates no conflict, but there must be conflict to evolve the best course of action. A change agent had the responsibility to propose alternatives as well as highlight consequential costs. A change agent controls natural conflict by balancing dominant forces regardless of their orientation.

An important part of the change agent's job is to balance the needs of all organizational elements without putting stumbling blocks in their path. Only in this way will individual creativeness and departmental initiative flourish. Change agents have to be constantly alert to the problems and the potential dangers of rampant internal conflict. They cannot relinquish the proper exercise of authority, and they must use their authority for the total corporate good.

Focus on Competition

Before any corporation can have external success it has to achieve some degree of internal tranquility. The magnitude and direction of internal conflict have to be recognized and dealt with. If conflict has been rampant within the organization for some time, department heads are probably ready to have some sort of order and stability imposed from above.

This is the time for the change agent to chart the course of future corporate action and the role of each department in achieving corporate goals. That is not to say the change agent can do it alone. Enlisting the support of key department heads for the total corporate good can be the beginning. And managerial job rotation can assist in squelching functional polarization.

But perhaps the greatest weapon in the hands of the change agent is a real or imagined external threat. Focusing on competitor's activities can get the whole organization pulling in the same direction. Production people will happily digest and attach a competitor's probable production techniques. Sales will happily analyze his marketing techniques for their strengths and weaknesses. During this analytical and introspective process, polarized functions will be joined for a common purpose. Then, too, during this process internal conflict can be made to look like a form of corporate treachery. Either of two arguments — the competitors are hot on our heels or we've got to catch up — can be used to refocus any functional outbursts.

The tendency to magnify competitors' strengths has to be controlled. Too often we view competitors with an awe that is unjustified and they may view us the same way. Although specific details and facts of competitors' operations may be hard to come by, a good deal of specific information can be gathered. The detailed and proper evaluation of such information is most important. The competitor's product itself is a veritable storehouse of information and should be treated the way an anthropologist treats an artifact from some ancient civilization. Just as the story of civilization can be recreated by critical analysis of remnants, so too a competitor's story can be largely told by his products.

The little that can be gleaned from a competitor's annual statements and reports should be used by the change agent to quantitatively identify areas of potential improvement. Likewise, ratio analysis of industry information can be most helpful in determining the relative position of companies in that industry.

Rather than concentrate on segments of a competitor's activities, the change agent puts together a total picture. From the interrelationship of competitive strategies and tactics in marketing, production, R&D, and the other functions involved, he then develops a corresponding set of productive and unifying strategies and tactics for his own company.

However, he knows it is not enough to imitate. Understanding competition is but a step in developing an organization that can react to change and be truly innovative. The change agent must guide and focus internal energies. He must control and direct conflict toward constructive ends and keep it from ripping the organization apart. Properly controlled, conflict can serve the organization by pointing the way toward profit and stimulating the company to excellence.

STIMULATING YOUR COMPANY TO EXCELLENCE

A vice president of a growing electronics firm visited a supplier of components to discuss possible price reductions. During the discussions the president of the components company said he couldn't supply the components at lower prices. In fact, he and his marketing people were considering raising prices. The usual reasons such as rising labor and materials costs were cited.

During a break in discussions the components president took the electronics vice president on a plant tour. Although many of the production operations were different, it was obvious to the vice presi-

dent that the people on the production line were
working as if someone had turned them on at slow
motion. The vice president was used to the brisk pace
at his own plant, and the difference was startling.
After returning to the president's office he asked
why the production workers were so slow.

"Oh, that. We know they don't put out a lot, but
what they do put out is the very best quality."

A company can live a long time with this kind of
creeping paralysis, particularly if it has a competitive
advantage such as patent protection or if competition
is limited in its industry. Nevertheless, the paralysis
will in time take its toll, especially in these dynamic
times.

Innovation and Creative Impatience

What does a change agent do if he observes these
symptoms? How can he help a company practice
preventive medicine to keep itself healthy? There are
many things he can do. For one thing, change agents
know that innovation and creative impatience are
becoming increasingly popular in running today's
businesses. Moreover, they know how to put innovation and impatience to work. There are better ways to
do almost everything. The problem is to determine
the best methods and then aggressively implement
them. Healthy businesses can stay healthy by creating
a climate that fosters innovation. Managers must be
imbued with a desire to play a greater role and must
be provided with a vehicle by which to achieve this
greater role. Further, they must be charged with the
responsibility for innovation.

All companies charge top management with total profit responsibility. Some companies even charge various management levels with a measure of profit responsibility consistent with authority. Rarely, however, do companies charge any managers outside of R&D with innovation responsibility. Profit responsibility without innovation responsibility is comparable to responsibility without authority. Future profits are based on innovation, and long-term corporate survival begins with innovation. Moreover, profitability in many companies rests solely on innovation advantage and disappears as soon as the innovation has become routine.

We usually associate innovation with research and development alone, though it may occur in production and marketing as well. A company outstanding in research and development but weak in innovative production and marketing will be outperformed by an organization with a high level of innovation in all three categories. But innovation does not just happen, it must be organized and deliberate in each of the basic areas of industrial life. It can be made manageable by stating business objectives and then planning strategies and tactics to meet these objectives. A corporate rating on an innovation scale might well serve as a barometer of corporate health.

One change agent who was with a large chemicals company called together R&D staff members with doctorates in chemistry for informal brainstorming sessions to develop new and unique marketing ideas. Another change agent brought together a group of corporate lawyers, engineers, and accountants in brainstorming sessions out of which an important new emphasis in product-production modularity for inventory reduction was evolved. Still another change agent used brainstorming sessions, executive rotation, and outside training consultants to develop an organized program of continuing innovation.

Making Use of Tension and Anxiety

Contrary to popular belief, tension and anxiety can be good for a company. Tension keeps the company from becoming complacent and a little anxiety brings into use talents and energies which are otherwise dormant. Tension and anxiety can stimulate interest in a company's day-to-day affairs, trigger achievement and innovation, and create a climate conducive to change.

One role of the change agent is to inject the proper quantities of tension and anxiety into the corporate bloodstream with tonic questions, which are similar to the seed-planting questions discussed in Chapter IV. Properly timed tonic questions can be invaluable in reawakening the corporate spirit. What does this company want as a minimum profit objective? Such a tonic question appeals to corporate self-interest and can cause a healthy reexamination of goals and objectives that have grown stale. More than one company has shifted into higher gear when it took the time to reconsider basic questions: Why are we in business? Where do we want the business to go? How are we going to get it where we want it to go?

Tonic questions can also appeal to a company's competitive spirit. Does this company want to set sales records or is it content to let the competition walk away with all the prizes? Well-placed questions such as these can help arouse a sleepy sales force. Tonic questions that focus on competition are particularly valuable not only because they appeal to everyone's fighting instinct but because competitors are usually highly visible targets.

But change agents do more than ask questions. They can stimulate anxiety by setting tight schedules for work completion. They can challenge an organization to plan and complete jobs by a set time, thus overcoming the temptation to procrastinate. Once the job is complete the change agent can quickly direct efforts to bigger jobs with more potential contribution. These are not artificially created jobs we're talking about; the only thing artificial is the time allowed for their completion. Artificially tight time limits will produce tension that can have a stimulating effect. But these time limits should not be confused with engineered work standards established for repetitive jobs.

Change agents know that organizations, like individual employees, need standards of performance to keep moving. One commonly used standard is ratio analysis, by which companies in an industry can measure themselves with respect to their competitors. Trade associations frequently collect and disseminate such information. All sorts of tonic questions pop up when one company compares itself to its competitors through such ratio analysis.

As a last resort, if there aren't enough tension-producing emergencies or problems a change agent may consider creating some. Artificial or simulated challenges are like fire drills that train personnel to cope with the real-life situation when it does occur and enable management to evaluate employee response under stress. Such exercises lose value if they can be distinguished from genuine challenges. In using artificial emergencies never underestimate the power of the grapevine in thwarting your purposes.

Tension and anxiety in controlled amounts provide the spur that causes innovation to happen. When there is no need for innovation the drive toward it is diminished; the organization can limp along doing what it has always done in the past.

Tension and anxiety should be carefully controlled—the pressure to innovate must be neither too high nor too low. If innovation is too easily achieved, innovators lose interest. On the other hand, excessive difficulty leads to frustration or desperation. Optimal pressure is attained when aspirations exceed achievements by a small amount.

Can You Afford to Be a Nice Guy?

In some businesses you just can't be a nice guy and survive; in others you can—up to a point. Patting an employee on the back and rewarding him is appropriate if such rewards are tied to profit achievement. It is the change agent who provides the guidance as to how nice you can afford to be.

Recently a company that had high-paid, happy employees went out of business. A significant factor in its failure was excessive labor costs. Now these ex-employees are no longer happy and neither are the former owners. For that matter, the customers are not happy either. Every company recognizes its responsibility for controlling costs to assure profits and business success. Change agents draw attention to another important responsibility—to provide employees with continued employment. The employee can have a job only if the business generates profits. What good are high wages if, because of them, a company has to go out of business? What good is a management that tolerates poor work methods, sets low goals, and gives little incentive for performance?

Certainly management must not accept mediocrity in the performance of others. Managers have to set high performance standards and demand that they be met. They have to guarantee the integrity of the organization through profit achievement. They also have to know where to draw the line in trying to be nice guys. The leadership exercised by management is the single most important factor in profit achievement, and how this leadership is exercised is critical. Managements that are actively working with their change agents and are vitally concerned with the day-to-day operations of the business are most successful.

IS YOUR COMPANY TAKING ENOUGH CHANCES?

When a request for additional record storage space worked its way to the president of a medium-size metalworking firm, the president exploded. "We need this space for products, not for records. Products make money for us; records don't. Besides, we already have too many records." Sound familiar? Many companies are in the same boat, and the problem is growing worse. Yet, as a rule, the records and papers generated by any business are crammed into inaccessible corners, and the president is unaware that there is a problem until the paper overflows into valuable space.

At the start, when a company probably has more space than it needs, it's easy to find a place for things that don't really have to be kept. During this time a pattern of retention is established that is difficult to change. Parkinson's law says that work expands to fill the time available for its completion. A physical chemistry law says something similar about the molecular dispersion of gases: Molecules of a gas expand to fill the volume the gas occupies. A corollary to these laws may well be that the files of a factory or office expand to fill the space available.

The Paperwork Explosion

Today we are faced with explosive growth not only in population but in paperwork. The reason most frequently given is that to operate in today's complex world, businesses need more facts and therefore more paper to put them on. Modern technology contributed its share. The paper-generating capabilities of computers began to have an impact in the late fifties. Now, even small computers spew forth more paper than a bank of executives can read in a lifetime. Even small companies find themselves buried under a mountain of reports—and reports on reports.

Perhaps the greatest threat to the average business has been the photocopying machine. Devices to copy documents can churn out as many as 3,600 copies an hour, with promises of even greater speeds to come. What's worse, they are often accessible to any clerk who decides to make copies of anything. Small wonder that a major automobile company recently installed locks on its photocopying machines.

With a stated need for more paper and the means to get it, the average business can drown in a sea of paper. In a large sense, the fact that companies are generating and saving a lot more paper is symptomatic of a deep-seated fear of taking chances. Yet, to combat this deluge, more and more companies are forced into the seemingly drastic tactic of taking more chances. Strangely, if company presidents were making decisions on what to keep and what to toss, companies would keep a lot less paper. The president's perspective makes him a better judge of the relative importance of sundry pieces of paper, and he is often more willing to take chances.

Every executive knows that business success often is based on a willingness to take a certain amount of chances; yet many are unwilling to do so. To discover the reasons we have to examine how some typical modern businesses evolved.

The Take-No-Chances Company

Somewhere in the humble beginnings of every business was an entrepreneur. He had enough guts to take chances, and he risked his time, talent, and money in a venture that perhaps others thought too risky. As the business grew he went on taking chances. He tried new products and new ideas. He charted a course that was often fraught with danger. The mistakes, and there were some, were offset by the successes.

As the business flourished, for better or worse he molded the organization in his own image. To achieve greater success the entrepreneur had to surround himself with assistants. But these men were cut from a different cloth. If they had been willing to take chances, they too would have become entrepreneurs. Because they were not so inclined, they sought out ways to protect themselves and their jobs in a corporate environment. Certain rules evolved—administrative rules of good conduct, if you will. Keep your desk orderly. Get to work on time. Keep copies of all memos. Route memos to your political friends whether they need them or not. Keep your shoulder to the wheel, your nose to the grindstone, and your ear to the ground. Above, all, *don't take chances.*

Such rules more often than not were the antithesis of the entrepreneur's approach to business. He didn't get to work on time. He was always early or he never left with the others. His desk— if he had one—was cluttered with sketches and notes and paraphernalia expressive of the creative mind. He hated paperwork with a passion. He was always bursting with things to be done, and paper got in his way. Yet he knew he needed an organization and so he built one. But it was difficult to attract people who would work in his dynamic shadow, and those he did attract were often weak. Although he was a technical or sales genius, his capability did not extend to developing the right kind of organization.

Paradoxically, his strength diminished his subordinates' tendency to take chances and increased their need to protect themselves. The more demanding and aggressive he was, the more the business became a one-man show. Subordinates wouldn't or couldn't trust their own judgment. Decisions had to be cleared with the entrepreneur, all major actions revolved around him, and he cursed his subordinates' weakness while relishing the belief that only he could do things right. His subordinates dared less as he demanded more, and the vicious cycle continued. Nor was the situation reversed if the organization outlived the entrepreneur. His modus operandi, for good or ill, was indelibly stamped into the fabric of the business.

The What-If Company

Many businesses justify their unwillingness to take chances by the what-if principle. Their controllers ask the question: "What if thus and so were to happen?" Then they build a system that is prepared to deal with this event. Indeed, many controllers proceed to the assumption that what could happen will happen. Although it's against their nature, controllers should be gamblers; they should concern themselves more with probability than with possibility.

One company kept duplicate records of *all* transactions in a remote location because destruction of the records in a fire would put the firm out of business. (The statistical chance that a fire will destroy all records is extremely low.) In time, the task of duplication, retention, and retrieval grew so costly and so time consuming that it had to be discontinued. Now only vital records are duplicated—and on microfilm.

Today, many companies have wisely concluded that business interruption insurance can spread the risk of major catastrophes and that selective records retention is enough to reconstruct basic business facts and customer accountability.

Legal advisers sometimes create monsters of records retention programs when they advise, and rightly so, that certain records be retained over a period covered by the statute of limitations. One business set out to keep copies of every delivery receipt (to prove delivery) and every invoice (to verify the items shipped) for seven years. At the end of the second year of operation a whole wing of the factory floor was filled with these records, and space was eventually leased at a local warehouse. Needless to say, the cost of storing these records was considerable.

The legal advice rendered in this instance was in answer to the question, "How long should we keep these records?" The answer was that in the event of a suit within the statute of limitations period to collect money due the firm it would have to prove what was delivered (the invoice) and by what means (the delivery receipt).

How often did this firm actually institute legal proceedings to collect money? As a practical matter, legal action was too costly because 98 percent of the firm's orders were under $100 in value. Customers with aged balances were subjected to a collection routine which was terminated when the account was turned over to a collection agency. Delivery records for recent orders were kept in a sales service department for easy reference, and if there was any question, a duplicate order was shipped. Orders with larger dollar value were shipped by truck because of their weight. A bill of lading was proof of delivery for a claim against the carrier in such instances.

Thus this management was fulfilling its legal obligations at the expense of its business obligations. Too often we follow legal advice to the letter without stopping to remember that an excellent attorney may be a poor businessman. It is incumbent upon management to make legal requirements and business requirements mesh into realistic programs.

Records retention programs usually are treated like poor relatives — leave them alone and maybe they won't bother you. Yet they are a good barometer of a company's willingness to take chances. Significantly, many companies have no formalized policies, perhaps because they don't want to commit themselves to a course of action that may prove embarrassing. Some enlightened companies base their records retention program on statistics and store records on a need-to-know basis.

In time all organizations begin to show signs of aging. Young, vigorous, aggressive organizations are not afraid to take chances. As they mature they have to take steps to retain their youthful vitality. Treatment begins with a change agent who can direct new blood and new ideas toward productive ends. A dynamic change agent brings about self-renewal by encouraging a let's-take-chances attitude throughout the company.

In concept, this attitude has changed our way of life. For example, the supermarket as we know it today resulted from a willingness to take chances. In the old-time grocery store the grocer obtained the items the customer asked for and served one customer at a time, which was slow and costly. In the supermarket, however, the burden of filling an order is on the customer. Self-service cuts labor costs, but it entails taking chances. For instance there is a higher incidence of theft and a smaller unit profit in supermarket operations. But taking a chance on a small unit profit and higher volumes is a reasonable one, as witness the large number of successful supermarket chains and the dwindling number of small independent grocers.

Taking chances through customer participation is used by change agents to lower costs. But in addition it lets the customer take part in the selection of his merchandise or in the development of his order. Participation reduces errors because the customer selects what he wants, and it increases sales not only because of lower prices but because of impulse buying, which is encouraged by merchandise displays and the customer traffic flow patterns.

Some mail-order houses ask the customer to fill out shipping labels as well as an order blank. Since these are used to pick, pack, and ship the order there is no chance of transcription errors in transferring data from an order to a label and little or no delay in getting the order shipped.

In another example of customer participation, an electronics firm used an incoming purchase order as its picking and shipping paper. Two copies of the purchase were made. One copy served as a packing list with the outgoing shipment. The second was sent to the receiving location to show that the merchandise had been shipped. The last copy was kept as a record of the shipment for billing purposes. With the order the customer received a packing slip, which was a photocopy of the original purchase order. Thus the supplier had little or no paperwork and the customer was spared the task of checking the packing slip against the original purchase order.

Developing a Let's-Take-Chances Attitude

Change agents have found other areas where it pays to take chances and where a company can save money by working smarter, not harder. These shortcuts can be creatively custom-tailored to suit the unique requirements of the change agent's firm.

Idea 1: Curb your controls. Companies afraid to take chances are inclined to apply controls until they are so tangled up in their own red tape that the controls have to be bypassed or entirely disregarded if anything is to be accomplished. What was begun as a controlled situation thus gets out of control because of the sheer bulk of the procedural apparatus.

Unhappily, top managers are often unaware that the procedural apparatus has collapsed. It would be wise for them to keep in mind that there are four distinct versions of any procedure: first, the way the procedures manual says it should be done; second, the way top management thinks it is being done; third, the way the supervisor thinks it is being done; and fourth, the way it is actually being done.

Paradoxically, a company with too many controls may be taking more chances than one with reasonable controls. When several control functions are established in a procedure, no group is directly responsible for error control. A few frequently audited controls are better than many that exist only in the procedures manual.

At one company, when an order was received it was assigned a job control number which was entered on the papers going to the manufacturing superintendent. The product was manufactured and moved to shipping where a delivery receipt was prepared. The delivery receipt had a different control number. After the job was delivered a copy of the delivery receipt was used to prepare an invoice. The invoice had still another control number. This numbering system was designed to give the highest degree of control possible.

To be sure that all jobs delivered were invoiced, a log of numbers was kept that referenced delivery receipts to invoices (log 1). To be sure that every job produced in the factory was delivered, a log was kept referencing job numbers to delivery receipt numbers (log 2). And to be sure all jobs manufactured were actually billed, a log was kept to reference job numbers back to invoice numbers (log 3).

This triple numbering system was developed early in the company's history when there were few jobs to keep track of. But as the business grew, the work involved in reconciling these control numbers was excessive. Posting to the three logs was months behind. Discrepancies were discovered too late to ascertain what had actually happened. Some jobs were delivered but never billed. Some jobs were manufactured but not delivered until an angry customer called to complain. The procedures remained chaotic as well as costly until a change agent designed a new system that eliminated the referencing logs, ended billing delays, and reduced the office staff by 30 percent. Now the company has enough control to be sure that every job delivered is billed.

Idea 2: Cutting corners with customers. Some companies make assumptions about what their customers want and then build far more refinements into their products than their customers require. These companies, usually engineering oriented in nature, try to design the best product possible but have little regard for end use or have a exaggerated view of the product's importance.

Sometimes parts are produced to a tolerance on one ten-thousandth of an inch when a lesser tolerance would suffice. And sometimes parts are forged or machined when a simple stamping would do the job at much lower cost. Value analysis, which looks at such questions as these, has become a valuable tool that could be applied more widely—for example, in analyzing the paperwork within and between companies.

Idea 3: Check your paper. Paperwork adds nothing to a product except cost. Cutting paperwork not only saves time and money but may also improve customer service. Experience has shown that the simpler the business system, the better it works. Simple systems are those that use the least paper and are most easily understood by the people who have to make them work.

Idea 4: Get things to work for you, not against you. Systems should be designed to serve more than one purpose and thus increase efficiency. For example, an account number that combines the zip code with a portion of the person's name will eliminate duplicate numbers for the same person and can also be used in sorting mail by geographical areas.

Color can also be convenient for identification and can have more than one use. For example, one mail-order company sent customers envelopes in one of five colors. When their orders were received the envelopes were sorted and processed by color—one for each day of the week—thus making it easy to spot any orders left over from the day before.

Idea 5: Use rubber stamps. Properly designed forms do a lot, but they can do more when combined with a rubber stamp. For example, one rubber stamp on the face of a purchase order can indicate acceptance and another can indicate rejection. Furthermore, the receiving department's purchase order copy can have appropriate quality control information entered in a space provided in the design of the stamp.

Idea 6: Take chances with less control. A mail-order company offered premium merchandise at a reduced rate for all customer orders above a minimum dollar value. There was no attempt to control coupon redemption since the sale price was equal to the cost price. Honoring all coupons avoided the cost of correspondence with those who did not comply with the offer and prevented customer ill will.

In another situation where merchandise was offered free to people who sent in coupons, a simplified control device was installed. Rather than checking the dollar value of related invoices, all coupons were honored. The first day of the promotion campaign a spotcheck was conducted and a cheater's chart was drawn up to determine the cheater ratio, but there were no other controls. Management was willing to stand the loss on the rare occasion when somebody applied for an unearned premium.

The same policy of taking chances holds true for complaints of nondelivery in many mail-order houses. Chances are that if you contact a mail-order sales service desk and say you never received an order, an interesting cost-cutting procedure will be set in motion. The first step is to determine that an order existed. If it did and was for a limited amount, a new order will be put through without verifying whether the original order was filled. Then your name will be entered on a record which identifies you as a complainer. The next time you register too many complaints your claims will no longer be honored.

Mail-order companies find that procedures such as these keep total costs to a minimum. However, additional safeguards may be installed. Perhaps you haven't received your shipment because of inadvertent delays. Immediate response to such complaints would result in double shipments. To avoid this they use delaying tactics. One is to send a double postcard explaining that the merchandise is on its way and asking the customer to mail the return postcard if the merchandise doesn't arrive.

As these examples demonstrate, the trick in taking chances is to balance the cost of control with what a business can reasonably expect to lose if no control exists. Too often, control-conscious businesses consider only the magnitude of potential loss. Such reasoning assumes that a disproportionate number of people will take advantage of them; yet any astute businessman knows that relatively few people will actually do so. This is particularly true when dealing with reputable business establishments.

BUILDING A CLIMATE FOR CHANGE

The words of the change agent of a large and successful company help to explain his company's success:

> Don't be afraid to make mistakes. Many companies are so paralyzed from the fear of making mistakes that they don't do the things they should; they don't try new and different ideas. They steadfastly refuse to change even though they know change is inevitable, so they get stale, and in this rapidly changing and competitive world of ours when you get stale, you're through.
>
> Risks are essential for business survival. And taking risks means you're going to make an occasional mistake. I watch my key executives to see which ones are making mistakes. If they're making too many, I try to help them develop better judgment. If they're not

making enough, I encourage them to try new and different approaches to our business. If they're not making any, I get rid of them. They are too conservative and will never make it in the long run, so why waste their time and ours. One of the most frustrating experiences is hiring a potentially capable risk taker and finding his habits and his fear of taking chances are so well ingrained that we can't break through.

What this change agent said was that he really doesn't want mistakes but he wants what mistakes can buy: a team of capable executives who have learned by making mistakes.

It Pays to Make Mistakes

Few companies encourage mistakes; what they do encourage is risk taking, and if in the process of taking risks a few mistakes are made, they feel it's well worth it. Nothing teaches a potential manager faster than the opportunity to make mistakes, and an astute manager will rarely repeat a mistake. Corporations geared for growth know the educational value of trial and error. They understand progress is made not necessarily by doing things we know well, but by doing *new* things.

All companies make mistakes, but few publicly admit to them. One never sees "costs of mistakes" on any profit and loss statement. Yet mistakes are a natural cost of doing business. In fact, businesses that make few mistakes may be caught in a form of business paralysis.

Business organizations are predisposed to assign

responsibility commensurate with authority. Thus the authority to do things and the possibility of doing them wrong are limited by one's position in the hierarchy. To put this another way, big mistakes are supposed to be made only by big men; little men should stop with little mistakes. When we pay more for jobs at the top, we're really paying for the ability and predisposition *not* to make mistakes. Although where one stands in the corporate structure depends on many things, it theoretically is based on simple economic and competitive propositions.

One such proposition is that the man least likely to make a mistake should rise to the top, and if he makes too many, a competitor ultimately replaces him. In actual practice, however, the corporate hierarchy is not a freely competitive society. Each individual is dependent on his superior and could hardly reveal that superior as inept without threatening himself in the process.

It is a widely held belief that good people, like the cream in milk, always rise to the top. But modern organizations have become so homogenized that the cream can't rise to the top—it can't even separate. In such structures individual progress often is no more than an endurance contest; as the Peter Principle puts it, people rise to their level of incompetence. And whatever the level, they are authorized to make mistakes in keeping with their responsibilities; more can be cause for severe discipline. With such organizational logic prevalent, it's no wonder many companies are "idea poor" and caught in the fear-of-mistake paralysis.

Mistakes are a natural and normal part of doing business. Indeed, it is mistakes in judgment, as well as human foibles and error, that relegate business to an art or a practice rather than a science.

In the practice of business, management requires controls to assure itself that each element stays within prescribed limits. If an element strays beyond the limit, certain warnings are sounded. First the warnings are heard by lower echelon management. If they go unheeded the warnings are heard by successively higher levels of management until they reach the top. But rarely do such warnings reach the top; they are designed to be caught by lower management for appropriate reaction and correction. Therein lies the control.

Consider the controls exercised by modern business: production and inventory control, quality control, budgeting and financial control, forms control. Now consider how such controls sound an alarm before the corporation gets into too much trouble. Properly structured managerial control reports allow lowest level managers to monitor actual operations. If operations are not kept in check, the next management level is advised by a similar reporting mechanism. Thus controls and the feedback from them provide a net whereby judgmental mistakes will be caught before they become a threat.

The organizational structure itself is designed to minimize risk. The management training process allows lower level managers to make relatively small decisions with small potential liability and limited risk. As the trainee proves capable of making bigger decisions, he is allowed to do so. In this way progressive companies encourage risk taking commensurate with a proven capability for making correct decisions.

The organization provides a built-in means of minimizing mistakes as well as mechanisms to prevent them from getting out of hand. In this way mistake control is similar to fire control. One of the basic rules in controlling fires is to localize them and keep them from spreading. Similarly, a basic rule in mistake control is to prevent the mistake potential from spreading.

For years, the military has used war games as a means of training young officers. These games, designed to simulate war conditions, provide a young officer with the chance to make decisions and mistakes without paying the penalties inflicted in real combat. Only relatively recently has business begun to use simulations and games as a means of training managers in decision making without incurring the costs of the inevitable mistakes.

Everyone would agree that planning is an important management responsibility, and some companies even define the management level by the amount of planning inherent in the job. Planning, itself a form of simulation, should include projections of what would happen under various conditions. Analysis of these projections allows us to select the best alternatives and thereby reduce the mistake potential.

Building a Judgment Capability

Management is engaged in the practice of running a business, and in so doing it makes decisions. Each decision is a judgment founded on the available facts.

Poor facts may cause poor judgments, but good facts are no guarantee of good judgments.

Some practitioners have a knack for quality decisions. Some can cut through a fog of ambiguity to spotlight relevant and meaningful data. But even the best are subject to judgmental errors. There is never enough information. Never can a bet be hedged in the right amounts. Never can risk be reduced to zero. All one can hope for is good data, proper hedges, and minimum risks. And even then every decision maker recognizes the inevitability of judgmental error.

So far we've talked about mistakes in judgment. But there is a basic distinction that must be made between judgmental mistakes and true errors. For example, it would be a judgmental mistake to agree to supply a customer with a product at a specified price over a period of time without due regard for labor or materials costs. The reason for such an agreement may be an assumption that labor or materials costs won't change significantly during the term of the contract or that excess capacity can be used because business is slow. No matter how reasonable an agreement may seem at the time, it could turn out to be a mistake in judgment. A change agent can do nothing to prevent judgmental mistakes other than to insist on rigorous analysis before decisions are made, not after. Indeed, it is incumbent upon him to encourage risk taking commensurate with the potential gain. Thus it can be said the change agent encourages mistakes.

True errors are usually less complex and hence easier to identify—for example, overbilling or underbilling a customer. Here we knew what was right but we did it wrong. No matter who caused the error or why it happened, the fact remains that from the customer's frame of reference we made an error. Because it's easy to identify such errors, it's also easy to get excited about them. It's easier to talk about errors than to do anything about them, and we do talk about them. Any worker would testify to the proposition that when things go well nobody seems to say much of anything, but make one small mistake and all hell breaks loose.

It's true that errors seem to get a disproportionate share of management attention, but management knows that recurrent errors can rack a corporation and shake it up. Once begun, errors have a nasty way of mushrooming. Since their cost and the problems they create can be staggering, it's no wonder that management leaps on the bandwagon whenever someone comes up with a proposal to control errors.

Guarding Against Overreactions

As a business grows, so too does the number of errors that occur. If the business grows rapidly, the error rate can grow exponentially. This is because, in the rush to meet business commitments, untrained personnel and untried procedures become the rule rather than the exception. As a result, in many businesses errors are limiting factors to further growth.

In an attempt to curtail errors and satisfy customers, some companies act on the assumption that the more people you have, the fewer errors you make. So they hire more people, and to their dismay, errors increase even further. Actually, more people just add to the confusion by magnifying the communication problem. Each person has to know what everyone else is doing, and each spends more time talking about the job than doing it.

A change agent will control the tendency to over-react to errors and will staff according to the number of errors his company can tolerate. He knows that an acceptable error rate is related to what an error costs, including the costs of correcting the error. Though errors involve a relatively small percentage of trans-actions, they represent a large percentage of the irritation and headache in an organization.

Once error costs are determined, the change agent can get some idea of the potential dollar saving that can result from improvement. Paradoxically, if error costs are relatively low, it may not pay to try to reduce them. However, direct costs alone may not be the sole criterion for such a decision since customer goodwill is involved.

Once the change agent knows his costs, an ideal error rate can be approximated for his business. This approximation balances the cost of controls to pre-vent errors and the cost of correcting errors when they occur. For example, the cost of correcting errors in an order filling operation includes the costs of the merchandise, the labor, and the paperwork as-sociated with shipping the correct items. The cost of prevention would be the cost of double-checking each order prior to shipment. (Even double-checking will not catch *all* errors.)

It is possible to identify an ideal error rate for each basic type of error and reduce each to a con-trollable level by spending money for controls. But each type requires a separate evaluation to see whether such controls are warranted. Also, an ideal error rate is not static; it changes as business conditions change. Certain business conditions warrant greater risk taking than others; and the more dynamic and changing businesses can expect higher error rates.

How the Change Agent Fights Errors

How does the change agent control errors? For one thing he determines how many complaints his company should tolerate before pressing the panic button, thus preventing the overcontrol of reacting to each and every complaint. He knows that needless or excessive control not only adds to costs but slows his company down and thereby impairs customer service. Determining an error allowance (the quantity of errors allowable for a given volume of business) beforehand prevents overreaction.

But the change agent does more. If errors are inherent in his kind of business he finds out what can be done to minimize them. He also error-proofs his firm by checking the following: Are procedures so complicated they cause errors? Are employees motivated to do their jobs right, or do they really care about what they are doing? Are employees capable of doing their jobs? Answers to such questions may reveal that changes are necessary. Eliminating the source of problems eliminates the problems. Armed with facts, the change agent can begin the process of change.

When a change agent is called upon to correct a

situation where errors have been rampant he does not point the finger of blame lest he make people defensive and uncooperative. Instead, he begins by setting up a procedure for tracking the error volume. Then he develops a means of identifying the people who are causing the errors, usually by assigning operator or checker codes. This step frequently pinpoints improper job training or poor personnel selection. An investigation by one change agent revealed that an employee who recently had been promoted to electronics color-code inspector was color-blind and was afraid to tell anyone. Without error control he could have gone undetected for months.

Another change agent kept an error incidence chart on his order filling and checking operations. He tallied customer complaints and posted them on a statistical quality control chart. When errors exceeded established high limits he investigated each complaint individually to identify the checker involved. This was a form of exception management since it was only done when errors exceeded the high limits. When errors were below the low limits for two consecutive reporting periods, his checkers received a bonus.

Your own operation and procedures best tell you what methods you must follow to bring about error control. The main idea is to take a hard look at the problem and make a beginning. If you don't, you are, in effect, committing another error.

IV

WORKING
WITH PEOPLE

ARE YOUR JOBS FIT FOR PEOPLE?

In September 1970 the Chicago Daily News Wire Services reported that the United Automobile Workers Union was offering a plan to fight job boredom and relieve the drudgery of assembly line workers. The plan proposed

> That teams of workers follow a new car down the assembly line working on the vehicle from start to finish. Workers now generally perform only one or two repetitive tasks. The UAW said its revolutionary proposal would make auto worker jobs more interesting and improve the quality of the product. Widespread boredom that comes from present work arrangements contributes to absenteeism and breakdowns in plant discipline.

Today, workers are different from preceding generations in life-style, values, and education. Yesterday's workers spent their lives in a single community and in one or two jobs, whereas today's workers move freely to new communities and new jobs. Today's worker has two and a half times the schooling of the average worker of 1900. Improved education and communication have made him more socially aware, more intractable, more determined to be liberated from the boredom of routine.

Young workers have rising expectations. They

feel they have a right to expect more from the work they do. The work ethic is changing, and people now want a greater range of satisfaction from their jobs. Personnel expert James L. Dougherty noted this change of attitude when he wrote:

> The semiskilled employee today surely knows that the *real work* is not done by himself. It was done by some planner who laid out the procedure or designed the machine and system. Observers see a deep problem in his loss of self-respect as a worker and of pride in work. Allied to this loss of pride in the jobs is the trend, over the years, toward less and less commitment by men and women to *work,* as a way of life.[1]

Today's more sophisticated workers would like a measure of self-fulfillment from their jobs. But because the typical job is highly structured and tedious, many of the young have become work dropouts. Some well-educated youths have turned to simpler lives to gain the fulfillment they cannot find in today's job market. Others take menial jobs merely to sustain themselves.

What's wrong with work and the way it's organized into jobs? Are the young too demanding? Do workers have a legitimate complaint if they derive no satisfaction from their jobs? What kinds of satisfaction is a worker entitled to? To understand the change in work attitudes, one has to take a fresh look at work itself.

---

[1] "What It Will Take to Supervise the Union-Free Employee in the Seventies," Dartnell Office Administration Service (July 1971).

Today's Workaday World

Most jobs today are merely an extension of concepts developed early in this century, when mass production techniques split jobs into highly repetitive and specialized tasks. The same techniques are still being used in most work situations. For example, most offices use assembly line concepts, splitting jobs into repetitive segments. It's no wonder the typical office is inefficient; its people suffer from the same boredom that afflicts automobile workers.

Work is boring because it leaves little room for self-expression and is too narrow and too specialized. Specialization was the key to higher productivity early in this century. But today's worker needs jobs that have been redesigned to overcome the boredom of specialization and to use his improved capabilities as a productive force.

For many businesses, lost profits attributable to the direct costs of overspecialization can be significant, but the hidden costs can be staggering. Consider the direct cost of overspecialization: salaries for too many people, each doing only a small part of the total job. Now consider the hidden costs. Splintered, repetitive jobs are tedious. Tedium leads to laxity. And when there is laxity quality suffers, errors increase, and customer complaints soar. Employees do not identify their small, repetitive jobs with the finished product, to say nothing of overall corporate goals. So they identify with their immediate work group and the goals of that group even if these goals are in conflict with company needs. The consequence? Productivity and worker performance suffer and costs soar.

Now we live in an age when jobs that on e encompassed many duties have been splintered to form many jobs, each requiring specialists with their own orientation and expertise. Among the factors working to cause increased job specialization was the more sophisticated environment, which triggered the need for more sophistication in business; for example, increasingly complex tax laws created a need for tax specialists; and federal, state, and local governmental regulatory bodies and agencies created a need for specialists to cope with the myriad legal and regulatory requirements.

In turn, greater employee sophistication, particularly at the professional and executive levels, triggered the needs for industrial relations specialists. Increased sophistication of stockholders and the general public created a need for corporate public relations specialists. Increased sophistication of buyers created the need for marketing specialists. And increasingly complex manufacturing and material technology created a host of other jobs.

The impetus toward specialization has other causes as well. For example, university training once followed the needs of business; that is, the demand for talent preceded the supply. But when this natural sequence of events is upset we have an oversupply of specialists. Such an oversupply is a by-product of the growing investments in research and development.

Not all the money being invested in research and development comes from the private sector of the economy. Government expenditures in the same area have added fuel to the fire. Universities have been the recipients of much of the money, and technically oriented industry has also received its share. The effort poured into such programs has given rise to new technologies and hence new jobs, first within the research organization and then in the business community. University training itself spawns new specialists, and business ultimately finds a place for them—whether it needs them or not. What is more, the government, as a growing sector of our economic life, not only parallels the university in its creation of specialists but causes industry to do the same.

Specialist Proliferation

When specialists penetrate one company in an industry, there is a chain reaction and every company wants one, thus creating an artificial demand. The pace of specialist proliferation is dependent on industrywide communication and the degree of competition within the industry. Professional societies do their part to spread the word about their own specialties, and trade magazines, technical shows, employment agencies, or the grapevine seem to do the trick for those without professional stature.

For example, when an operations researcher was hired by a leading soap company, other soap companies reacted fast. A perfunctory check revealed that nobody in these companies knew what operations research was, let alone what it could do. In the absence of any reason why they shouldn't, they began their search for these specialists. When this happens the specialists reap the benefits of increased wages based on artifical demand, but the companies derived little or no benefit because they are not equipped to use the talents effectively.

Yet specialization is inevitable, even in a static or depressed business, because the business environment demands it. This has nothing to do with the economy; it has to do with technological change, which demands changes in labor specialization. As a nation becomes more technically proficient, its labor force inevitably becomes more specialized.

The Diminishing Returns of Specialization

Labor specialization can be beneficial, but there is a point beyond which overspecialization creates problems and increases cost. This was well illustrated in a guitar manufacturing plant where workers on an assembly line were assigned highly specialized tasks. One worker affixed the neck to the guitar body; another screwed the hardware to the neck; another mounted the strings; another tightened the screws and strings; and still another tuned the instrument.

Productivity was high since each person was a specialist in assembling a portion of the guitar. However, there were frequent quality problems, and none of the assemblers felt individually responsible for the quality of the complete guitar since each had had a very small part to play in the total assembly.

Reverse specialization was tried in this case. The work was divided into separate work stations, special work benches were installed, and the assemblers were trained to put together the entire guitar and were charged with responsibility for quality. Because each became a specialist in the total assembly job, he developed a pride in accomplishment. As a result, quality improved and productivity increased.

Shaping Jobs to Fit People

Like products, businesses too can suffer from an excess of specialization. The change agent is particularly valuable here because he is adept at spotting overspecialization as a symptom of too much change, weighing its overall impact and assessing alternative courses of action. What can the change agent do? He can shape jobs to fit people instead of trying to make people fit jobs.

As a beginning, he can let employees know how their jobs relate to the company's product or service. If there is glamor in the product and some of the glamor rubs off on individual jobs, so much the better. But even routine work on the most mundane product can be glamorized by a creative change agent. It's important to show how a particular job enables the company to fulfill its mission. With this knowledge the employee can see the big picture and know how his effort contributes to the total effort of the corporation.

Through a planned training effort, the change agent can make generalists out of specialists. Organized job rotation is a significant step in this regard. Another is job enlargement, as was done with

116

the assemblers in the guitar company. The employee benefits from job enlargement because his job is more interesting and satisfying; the company benefits because the employee can now handle additional tasks.

The change agent also considers combining overlapping specialties. First, he ascertains how many people are doing similar things. Then he considers the benefits to be derived from combining these jobs or people in some new way. He knows that grouping related tasks under a common head can eliminate duplication of effort. Once this is done he can broaden each person's job assignments.

The change agent fights the trend toward hiring more specialists just because the competition is doing it. Before beginning a job search for new specialists he determines how they will affect the organization, who they will work with, and what kinds of work they will be doing. Perhaps it would be better not to bring in outside specialists but to implement a training program which will add to the effectiveness of existing employees and spur them on to greater achievements. Or perhaps a team effort will improve group morale and encourage creativity in addition to enlarging jobs.

Many social scientists are now saying that work is a game for the worker, in the sense of a developed pattern of social action and counteraction. The object of the game is for each person to protect his own self-esteem. Boring, uninteresting, socially unimportant, and meaningless work tends to undermine it. And the worker gets back at his employer with absenteeism, careless workmanship, slowdowns, and pilfering. To increase the worker's sense of self-value, the change agent can rebuild jobs to make them more complex and more challenging; enlarge jobs to encompass more of the steps in the whole process; rotate employees through a variety of jobs; and involve employees in the planning of their own work.

Also important in building an employee's sense of self-worth is a seeming trifle that is often overlooked: recognition for a job well done. William James said, "The deepest drive in human nature is the desire to be appreciated." All of us know the satisfaction we derive from doing something well. But the thing we remember most and derive the most satisfaction from is knowing that someone appreciated what we did. The value of a job well done is enhanced when it is shared and appreciated.

All workers have a range of satisfaction they need from their jobs. Typical individual needs are:

Doing something worthwhile (goal)
Trusting in leadership (respect, confidence)
Doing one's share (participation, achievement)
Having a sense of counting for something (recognition, appreciation)
Making a decent living (fair pay)
Having a chance to get somewhere (opportunity)
Having a safe future (security)
Knowing what's going on (communication)
Having decent conditions at work (environment)

These needs apply to all workers regardless of position. Scientists have found that when one particular need is threatened it becomes more important than the others. For example, job security is not a significant factor when jobs are easy to obtain, but it becomes significant when unemployment is high and remains so until the threat has subsided. Individual needs are dynamic, not static. Not only do these needs vary in importance among individuals, but their relative importance shifts as people mature and as their environment changes.

When a job does not satisfy a worker's needs, he may devote a great deal of energy and enthusiasm to negative satisfactions: striking back at the system, creating or passing on rumors, downgrading his leadership. These negative satisfiers become part of daily work life when employees have no employment alternative. They exist in all organizations to some degree. Negative satisfiers do not necessarily entail overt action on the part of the employee, nor are they deliberate acts of sabotage. Paradoxically, the worker is often unaware that he is giving expression to his frustration by displaying troublesome or uncooperative behavior.

Of course, if the frustration level is high enough, employees are always free to quit. But often they feel locked in by circumstances beyond their control. They may have seniority which they feel they can't afford to lose, or their skill may be limited to a particular business or industry. They may work in a community where alternative jobs are scarce. They may view alternative jobs as not much of an improvement, or starting all over again somewhere else may be distasteful. In the face of such obstacles, it is easier to keep the job and settle for negative satisfactions or seek satisfaction outside the job.

From the organization's view, the employees'

search for other outlets for their energies and talent is a waste of human resources. The change agent has the unique opportunity of bridging the gap between the needs of people and the needs of the organization. Fortunately, there is no inconsistency between individual and organizational needs, as is evident from the aforementioned list. High employee morale is a by-product of sound organization and administration. Good morale and good results are two aspects of the same thing—sound organization and capable leadership.

Change agents have to cut across functional barriers so that work can be made more meaningful to workers, managers, and consumers. Workers should participate in work planning, using their creative skills to improve what they do and the way that they do it. When necessary, workers should be trained to use their creative abilities. Coincident with training, a climate for change has to be cultivated so new ideas can be realistically evaluated and then acted upon.

Other steps can be taken to harness the creative talents of employees. New life can be given to the dormant suggestion box. Or a sales campaign of sorts can be launched to focus excitement and sell employees on improving their own work. Texas Instruments, Motorola, and others have used team work/work team concepts to imbue employees with a sense of belonging to a cohesive productive force. This has made employees more concerned and more dedicated. Office workers, who have been exempt from the more traditional productivity improvement techniques, are no exception. The work team concept has been applied to white collar workers in an effort to develop better ways of accomplishing work and to combat rising clerical costs.[2]

The value of employee participation isn't limited to business organizations. A survey of 16 hospitals concluded that patient care can be vastly improved if hospital employees participate in matters affecting their jobs.[3] Other studies in public management and government have concluded that employee participation is a vital ingredient of meaningful change. Traditional approaches to public management have been based on command systems. A newer technique, organization development, seeks to bring about change and improvement by involving members of the organization in problem analysis and planning.[4]

The TRW Systems Company has put behavioral science principles to work. Sheldon A. Davis of TRW listed the following guidelines for success in employee-employer relations:

1. The individual is important.
2. Attract the best people, give them the best working conditions, and provide them with challenging assignments.

---

[2] Lee Grossman, "Work Teams Bring Flexibility to Office Methods," *The Office* (September 1968), pp. 57–63.
[3] Robert C. Holloway and Wallace C. Lonegan, "A Survey Program for Management and Organization Development," *Hospitals* (August 16, 1968), pp. 59–65.
[4] William B. Eddy, "Beyond Behavioralism? Organization Development in Public Management," *Public Personnel Review* (July 1970), pp. 169–173.

3. Trust individuals with minimum rules and controls.

4. Design policies and procedures to be a platform from which the individual operates, rather than a set of rules within which he must confine himself.

5. Give individuals too much responsibility too soon. Stretch them for their growth and outstanding performance.

6. Develop a society of peers rather than a rigid hierarchy. Managers shouldn't use rank as a barrier between themselves and others at lower levels of the organization.

7. Delegate a great deal downward through the organization so a large number of people end up with responsible tasks.

8. Work ought to be personally rewarding, meaningful, and fun. Jobs should be seen as making a significant contribution to important advances in society.[5]

TRW and Texas Instruments are sophisticated, technologically oriented companies geared to rapid change. By and large, their employees are highly skilled and well educated. One could argue that this kind of people and this kind of work are conducive to maximum employee freedom. The argument is correct, but that is not the point. The point is that all organizations will have to become like these companies to some degree. Rigid organizations with typi-

[5] For more detail on the TRW philosophy see Warren G. Bennis, K.D Benne, and R. Chin, eds., *The Planning of Change: Readings in the Applied Behavioral Sciences* (New York: Holt, Rinehart and Winston, 1961), p. 369.

cal hierarchies may survive for the moment, but what about tomorrow? Rigidity must give way to change or there will be no tomorrow for them, and companies like TRW can serve as their model.

PLANTING THE SEEDS OF THOUGHT

The talent and potential that every organization has is a tremendous reservoir that management can harness to the needs of the corporation. The problem for change agents, more often than not, lies in finding out how to go about harnessing this talent and potential.

Successful change agents subscribe to the belief that the motivation of others—that is, getting others to do things—is a key responsibility. Not only must they communicate and provide an environment where there are sufficient incentives, but they must also provide motivation so work is done on time in reasonable quantities.

Some approach motivation through the side door. They say that to motivate people is to let them participate in decision making. Then, after the decision has been reached, *they* will be responsible for carrying the program forward.

The participation concept works well at times. It's like motherhood; who can argue against it? But sometimes people dream up the wrong ideas. Or, what is worse, they don't dream up any ideas at all. An astute advertising executive once said: "Give us good publicity. Or give us bad publicity, if you must. But, above all, give us publicity." Similarly, poor ideas are better than none at all. Poor ideas can be redirected, sent back for review, or quietly scuttled. But an absence of ideas is a barren wilderness.

Breaking the Idea Barrier

Some change agents have found a way to stimulate thought in "seed planting," which they use to harness talent, motivate, overcome indifference, and break the idea barrier. Seed planting is the gentle art of getting others to come up with ideas. It is a means of focusing attention on specific needs or problems. After a seed is planted there is a reaction time when mental wheels turn and thought processes are busy. Then, finally, ideas sprout forth.

To some this waiting period seems interminable, particularly when time is of the essence. But change agents who plant seeds must be prepared to wait for them to take root. In doing so, they balance the need to do something now against the longer range goal of developing people.

Although the waiting is long, people grow and develop when they create their own ideas; they reach their full potential when they are encouraged to think and to expand their horizons. And in the process the corporation benefits from having more productive and concerned employees whose talents are fully utilized, and the employees achieve satisfaction and fulfillment from a job well done.

When the seed of an idea is planted it may not grow in the way the change agent expects. Soil conditions, climate, and environment shape its growth, just as people are shaped by their environment, education, and training. What is more, growth takes time. Remember how long it takes for children to acquire basic skills. And remember that the kind of growth we're talking about may have been actively discouraged in early educational experiences, which, not uncommonly, are designed to impart uniformity, not creativity, in thought as well as in actions.

Planting, Nurturing, and Harvesting Techniques

Seed planting is more productive when it is well organized than when it is haphazard. A farmer sows seeds in a pattern based on the contour of the land and the soil's fertility as well as the farm equipment. So, too, in corporate seed planting the pattern depends on the corporate structure. A number of techniques are available to improve the crop yield.

In seed planting to stimulate thought, direct action is to be avoided. Don't give direct orders or make direct suggestions; nothing kills creative thought faster. A question, a comment, even a facial expression can implant the seed of an idea. The seed planter acts as a catalyst, but things ultimately have to be done by others. They produce the ideas, and make them work.

The fishing technique. Seed planting is one technique for stimulating ideas; a more indirect approach is the fishing technique. Suppose you are assigned the task of determining how well a plant manager is doing his job. Suppose also you have no prior knowledge about the technical aspects of his job. After a brief tour of the facility you ask, "Are things always this way?" This is a fishing question. Note that the question is directed to the stability of operations, not the manager's ability.

His response is the key to your next move. If he says yes, more probing is in order. If he becomes defensive he probably is assuming you see the same flaws that he sees. The trick now is to find out what he sees wrong. Properly structured, well-timed questions will elicit revealing answers.

If he goes into detail about what he has to put up with, he may be looking for sympathy or a pat on the back. A few words of understanding and support or a comment about your similar plight (real or imagined) will make him responsive. Note that in fishing you cast your lure into the waters. What bites and how successful you are in the ensuing encounter depend largely on your skill and tact. The fact that you know nothing about the manager's operations means you have no preconceived notions and are free to concentrate on getting the answers.

Once fishing has begun, listen carefully. What the manager says and the way he says it can be important clues to what he's really thinking. Some managers may be reticent about discussing their operations in detail. Some may deny the existence of difficulties. But you can be sure they've got problems. Plant managers don't command the salaries they do for nothing.

If time is on your side don't push the issue; when you see him again a more specific approach can be used. For example: "The work methods on the line look good, but maybe there's room for improvement." Then you can ask "What do you think?"—a question that is one of the best lures known to mankind.

Direct confrontation. The direct confrontation technique, as its name implies, uses the question format of the fishing technique, but the question is much more to the point—for example, "How can we improve?" Such a question is a powerful seed that can yield a bountiful harvest of ideas by focusing attention on a specific area of interest. In doing so, you lose the peripheral and sometimes valuable information that one gains from fishing. But focusing in this manner avoids the qualifying diplomatic remarks and may get results.

Making the question even more specific — "Would an automated widget cutter be of any help in your operation?"—is a way of zeroing in on a specific area in the line. This approach is particularly good with unsophisticated personnel.

Rocking the boat. When fishing or direct confrontation technique won't work, more drastic measures are in order. Diametrically opposed to the diplomatic fishing technique is rocking the boat. This technique can be successful in stimulating ideas, but it is drastic and upsetting, and it should be used only as a last resort.

Rocking the boat is a tricky business. You want to rock it enough to accomplish your purpose but not enough to make waves that will swamp you in the process. A dramatic boat-rocking statement is: "The productivity of your operation has dropped by X

127

percent since March. How do you propose to turn it around?" If you smile when you say this, he'll remember the smile and may even improve the operation.

Still another boat-rocking approach is to make raw comparisons. For example, "Your operation is the only one that has failed to improve productivity since March." No one who is faced with a challenge of this sort is likely to be lethargic or indifferent, and that's half the battle. Rocking the boat is at best a hit-or-miss proposition and as such should be used only in emergencies.

Watch your timing. Effective seed planting depends on timing. After a spell of trouble everybody is ready to do something and penetrating questions of the what-if variety serve to get things moving in the right direction, especially in a brainstorming session. Guiding such group discussions is like running before the wind in a small sailboat. It takes skilled seamanship to bring the best ideas home to port.

Once the seeds have been planted it's important to neglect the seed bed—without feeling guilty. It's all too easy to worry about progress. Those sufficiently bothered take the bull by the horns and ram their ideas home, often over the objections of the very people they are trying to develop. Seed planting can be used to get people to think, and intelligent neglect will give the seeds time to germinate. In the process you will sharpen your own ability to listen and to manage the work of others. Create a climate that encourages growth in people and nurture ideas in the early stages until they ripen and bear fruit. When ideas are suggested, congratulate employees on their contributions. Employees who are armed with their own ideas and encouraged by a permissive climate will make their ideas pay off.

————————

GETTING PEOPLE TO THINK PROFIT

Once there was an owner of a small manufacturing business who was troubled because nuts, bolts, and assorted small parts were often left lying on the factory floor. One day he walked to the center of the assembly area, took out a roll of dimes, unwrapped it, tossed the coins into the air, watched while they rolled every which way, then calmly turned around and walked back to his office, leaving the assemblers and foreman to pick up the dimes and grumble that the boss had gone off his rocker.

The next day the president called a meeting of the assembly area employees. "By now you're all wondering what made me throw money around the assembly floor," he said. "No, I'm not off my rocker, I'm trying to impress you with the simple fact that we have a problem."

"Every day when I come out to the manufacturing area and to this assembly area I see assorted parts lying on the floor, and nobody bothers to pick them up. These parts represent money out of our pockets. Every time we fail to pick up a nut or a bolt or a cotter pin we are throwing money away, just as I threw money away yesterday."

129

A Lesson in Profit

In his own way this president was trying to teach his employees to think profit. It is easy for employees to disassociate themselves from a basic goal of every company: the goal of earning a profit.

People don't automatically think about the cost of the things they waste, especially when they are surrounded by evidence of waste. An employee may be quite concerned about where the dollars go when he is spending his own hard-earned money. But his employer's money is another matter; there seems to be a never-ending supply of that. No wonder our business bankruptcy is so high.

Profit is not a dirty word. It is a very necessary ingredient of corporate survival. Getting employees to keep this fact in the forefront can be a difficult task. However, a creative change agent can do many things to make employees think profit. One way is by developing a get-into-business-for-yourself feeling. Many employees do not associate their own goals with the goals of the business in which they work. To think profit, it is important that the employees develop a proprietary interest in the business and feel that if it succeeds, they will succeed.

If an employee were to leave and open up his own restaurant, he would see to it that his people worked diligently at all times, that his lights were turned off at closing time, that employees weren't putting too much soap in the dishwasher, that the food portions were controlled, and that the quality of the food was up to *his* standard of excellence. The change agent's task is to instill this same concern in each employee and keep him from feeling like a small cog in a very large machine. To do this he uses techniques designed specifically to make the employee feel that he is very much a part of the business. At the lower managerial levels particularly, change agents are increasing their use of participative management concepts.

Foremost in participative management techniques today is participative budgeting, which lets employees take part in setting budgetary goals and gets them concerned about the cost aspects of their job.

Budgets as Motivators

Meaningful participation in establishing budgetary goals goes a long way to encourage employee cooperation. A give-and-take atmosphere in setting these goals can make the employee understand the company's objectives and how he can help to meet them. Employees will tend to aim high if given an opportunity to set their own standards.

A budget can act as a motivating force and can induce employees to perform better. But if its aims and goals are too easy to attain, employees will produce below their capacities. Also important is feedback on how well the company is doing in meeting its goals. Failure to communicate information on results not only adversely affects performance but is also bad for morale. Letting your people know how they've done to date and what they should do in the future enhances the possibility of meeting your budgeted goals.

If there is little or no feedback on how they're

doing, employees will feel that management doesn't really care about their participation and that all the talk about participative budgeting was just a sham. Some managers think they should tell employees how things are going only as long as they're going well. But as soon as the picture darkens a little they shut off the flow of information. Paradoxically, communication should be increased rather than decreased when things are bad. It always amazes managers to see how well their people respond in an emergency. But they can only respond if you give them the opportunity.

Just as it's necessary that middle and lower management participate in the budget process, it's imperative that top management be actively involved and not merely shunt the responsibility off on the change agent. If top management indicates a lack of interest, this will be reflected throughout the organization. But if the change agent and top management work together they can have a stimulating influence by asking meaningful questions, suggesting alternative courses of action, and clarifying objectives.

The Profit Center

Closely associated with participative budgeting is the profit center—often called cost center in industry. The profit center's costs are subject to close control, but this control traditionally has been negative in that performance is measured historically and cost allocations are often inequitable. Although trend information can be significant, frequent changes in production techniques and product mix render historical comparisons unreliable.

Because the profit center is in effect in business for itself, it can be a powerful means of stimulating interest and control over the costs incurred in each segment of a business. Developing the think profit attitude is a problem of stimulating many little businesses within the framework of one big business. This means that profit centers have to operate on a businesslike basis. One way of doing this is to let each profit center generate income by selling its product or service.

The procedure goes like this. The product of each profit center is "sold" to the next department or profit center, which in turn treats the transaction as a purchase of raw materials. Each profit center has the option of going to outside vendors for the same raw materials. This competitive "purchasing" is a stimulating lesson in comparative costs. Sometimes, the price of a profit center's prduct is determined by "value added" considerations. Either method (sales value or value added) allows the profit center to generate income as well as costs. Thus it is effectively in business for itself since it can produce a meaningful income statement.

Now the change agent applies breakeven analysis to each profit center in order to develop flexible income and expense projections under assumed conditions as well as under alternative managerial programs. This helps him to analyze volume, prices, costs, and product mix, and relate this information between profit centers in an integrated manner.

Breakeven analysis also enables him to anticipate the impact of proposed changes before they are made.

Guided by recent behavioral science findings, change agents are trying other techniques to get people to think profit. For example, some are encouraging employees to disregard the chain of command and communicate directly with any manager in the organization. In many instances, this freedom does not extend to lower echelon workers but is limited to managers. However, in a growing number of companies, all employees are being granted greater freedom.

Creating Profit Excitement

To create real profit excitement the change agent has to open up new lines of communication. We display banners and repeat slogans for a quality control campaign or a safety campaign. But how many companies have ever gone on a profit campaign? Profit is as worthy an objective as quality or safety. Certainly without it, safety and quality notwithstanding, a firm will soon be out of business.

To get employees thinking about profit, one change agent collected all the wasted paper and envelopes from a day's run in an envelope manufacturing company and suspended this waste from the ceiling in a fishnet. A contest was held and Thanksgiving turkeys were offered as prizes for the three employees who came closest in guessing the dollar value of this one day's scrap if it were converted into finished product.

This way of getting employees to think profit had several purposes. First of all, the change agent was trying to reduce the amount of scrap that was being generated in the plant each day by dramatizing its sheer volume. Second, he wanted to emphasize the dollar value of this scrap and what it meant to the company in terms of profit and to the employees in terms of job security. Finally, he wanted to stir up some excitement about the company goal of reducing waste.

Another change agent put new life into a dormant suggestions program by converting from a cash award to an award of S&H green stamps. And yet another change agent created profit excitement by throwing a profit party. He organized games such as "pin the profit on the worker," which were similar to brainstorming. However, he opened the door to even wilder (and potentially better) ideas when he used the framework of a profit party since the party atmosphere broke down normal inhibitions. He also had a profit queen elected for the party. Appropriately, the costume for the profit queen was greenbacks.

Total Profit Training

Change agents use various approaches to get people to think profit and be concerned about costs. However, just being concerned about costs and thinking about profit are not enough. There has to be action to reduce costs and achieve more profit. And before there can be action there must be training, preferably in the form of seminars that teach fundamental profit concepts and what can be done on a practical basis to improve a company's profit position.

A meaningful total profit training program, tailored for a specific business, is the best form of profit insurance. For companies that are barely managing to limp along, such a program is long overdue. For companies earning a small profit it will help to boost that profit. And for companies enjoying a comfortable profit it will insure continued success.

Many training programs will help employees do their jobs better, among them job instruction training and value analysis training. However, before proceeding with specific techniques for profit improvement, it is desirable to have a thorough understanding of basic profit concepts. Too many companies embark upon a specific profit improvement training program without relating this training to the overall corporate profit objectives. A total profit training program begins with basic cost and profit relationships and makes participants aware of the big profit picture before zeroing in on profit enhancement techniques.

Everyone has some understanding of costs and profits but many people don't understand how the two are connected. Discussion in the training program focuses employee attention on some things that have long been taken for granted. For example, employees rarely give any thought to the cost of maintaining the factory or office space in which they work. Only when they themselves determine the cost factor of such items as rent, heat, light, and insurance per square foot does the cost and profit message really become meaningful to them. It's one thing to have someone tell you what your overhead costs are, it's quite another thing to find out these costs for yourself.

After basic cost and profit relationships are understood they have to be related to volume. This is most dramatically accomplished by means of a breakeven chart. Few people really know how it works or understand its value in profit planning. Learning to develop and work with a breakeven chart goes a long way in clarifying the relationship between profit and costs as well as the employees' role in this relationship.

Finally, a training vehicle is needed to tie together all that has been learned and to relate these concepts to real life. This vehicle is simulation: running a fictional company in competition with other companies with the expressed purpose of achieving maximum profit. This requires planning and decision making skills based on the cost and profit relationships that participants themselves developed early in the training sessions.

After a series of seminar sessions, participants begin to understand the problems faced by top management every day and also come to realize the need for profit and appreciate the effort required to achieve it. Only after there is thorough understanding of profit concepts should training in specific profit improvement techniques begin. Such training will then have heightened purpose and acceptance.

Seminar training can be an instrument for changing supervisors' viewpoints, values, and approaches to problems. The classroom attitude carries the job so that suggestions from employees or change agents are much more readily acted upon. Cooperation developed in a classroom seminar environment can be translated into meaningful action and cooperation in every profit endeavor.

V

SELLING CHANGE

STRATEGIES FOR SELLING CHANGE

Resistance to change is like sales resistance—for those who seek to bring about change, it is something to be overcome. For those upon whom the change is to be imposed, resistance is a natural defensive mechanism. At one time or another each of us plays both roles—the changer and the one on whom change is imposed. The changer is an active role; the other, usually passive. Role switching may give each new insight, but in any given situation the roles are clear and the lines of resistance harden quickly.

What to do about it remains the question. Like the weather, everybody talks about resistance to change but few do anything about it. Traditionalists will tell you it comes from fear of the unknown, but change concerns the future and the future is never known in advance. Indeed, explaining change often serves only to stiffen resistance. Yet involvement or participation in bringing about change appears to be one of the keys to success. Active participation can remove some of the fears, but this leads to the next problem: how to get that participation.

Some people are convinced that management support will encourage participation down the line. Even if this were true, how does one go about getting management support? More important, how does one get more than lip service when management itself is faced with a multitude of other problems, not the least of which is a broad spectrum of changes triggered by our age of change? More than likely, management support alone won't generate enough participation. Something more is required.

So overcoming resistance depended on removing fear of the unknown, which depended on participation, which in turn depended on management support, which probably, in the last analysis, is not enough to do the job. What is needed is a strategy to sell change, for change has to be sold. And the strategy must come from the changer himself.

The first phase in selling change entails fact gathering and analysis and the development of a specific proposal. There is no substitute for hard work in digging out the facts. The proposal will be founded on these facts, and anything built on a weak foundation will eventually crumble. The art of fact gathering includes knowing where to look for information and how to ask questions that will reveal the things you want to know, and the more you do it the sharper your fact-gathering ability becomes.

Once the relevant facts are gathered, analysis can begin. The interpretation and analysis of these facts and the subsequent development of a specific proposal rest on the combined skills of everyone involved in the study.

Many technically proficient analysts proceed through the fact gathering and analysis only to stop short of the most important ingredient—a strategy to get their change accepted—or arrive at premature change proposals. The best strategy once the facts are gathered and analyzed is to develop several tentative alternative solutions, documenting the advantages and disadvantages of each. These alternatives can then be used later to role play and presell a mutually agreeable change. We'll look at how this is done later. The important point to remember now is to develop a variety of change ideas, but not get married to any one of them.

Total Change Strategy

An important step in developing a total change strategy is to look at a change as if you were seeing it for the first time. From this vantage point, put the essence of the proposal on paper in a single sentence or a short paragraph. If you can't express the overall change succinctly, you haven't thought it through. In that event it can be developed further by asking: Why is it necessary? Who will it affect? Who will implement it? What are its benefits? What are its negative features? Do the negative features outweigh the advantages? Who will be the strongest supporter, and why?

Charles G. Mortimer, former chairman of General Foods, once explained the importance of thinking a thing through before risking exposure.

> There are three stages of thinking. The first stage is thinking about a problem, plan, or project. Sometimes we do this for years, without getting any benefit whatsoever from the mental energy we expend, because we do nothing about it.
>
> The second stage is thinking into the problem, plan, or

project. This entails bringing all our imagination, our resourcefulness, our inventiveness to bear.

The third stage is thinking through. This involves enlisting our very best judgment with respect to every phase and feature of the plan or project. It means facing realities, assaying the possibilities of failure, planning our attack, and organizing everything so carefully that no one will have to check up on us.[1]

Thinking through requires that we develop a strategy to go along with the change itself; otherwise it will gather dust in some corner of the corporation because no one promoted it. The first step in developing a successful strategy is to consider your company's change history. Every company has a certain propensity for change. Technologically oriented companies are comfortable with high change rates because they attract the kinds of people who are not disconcerted by rapid change. On the other hand, companies with more static markets, product lines, or production processes are less amenable to change. Their people are emotionally locked into present practices and may offer a high degree of resistance even when the company's very survival is at stake.

Thus each company has an environment that will foster or reject change, and each has a history of dealing with change. The environment has conditioned people to respond in certain ways when new changes are suggested. Checking the record of ear-

[1] Robert J. Tiernan, "Ideas—10 Ways to Sell Them," *Nation's Business* (June 1965), p. 85.

lier successes will yield important clues to the strategy that will be successful in the future. Particularly important is an understanding of the factors that make for success or failure. If a change is to stand any chance at all it will have to avoid repeating the mistakes of the past.

Change dictated by top management edict is called legislated change. Tightly controlled small companies with flat organization structures can impose change in this way. But for the most part top management legislates broad policy and then holds middle management responsible for implementation. In larger companies, policy changes are often distorted by the time their practical effects reach operating personnel. This is, for the most part, a communication problem reminiscent of the popular parlor game of lining up a group of people, whispering a story to the person at one end, having it transmitted from one to another down the line to the last person, then comparing his version with the original. Rarely do the two versions bear any similarity.

Even in companies with good communication networks, the impact of legislated change on each department can never be totally anticipated. Moreover, every plan has to allow room to maneuver so it can be smoothly incorporated into work requirements, personnel availability, and so on. Since top managers can't predict a change's impact with reasonable accuracy, they can only state broad policy guidelines and then leave it to the individual department managers to make the policy work. Small wonder that some managers are frustrated by what they see as a slow-moving, ponderous organizational apparatus incapable of responding to genuine company needs.

The Role of Change Agents

Bringing about meaningful change in today's complex world is a job for a staff specialist—the change agent—who is charged with the responsibility not only for initiating change, but also for analyzing facts and coming up with the best kinds of change, taking into consideration the uniqueness of the company, its people, and other resources.

If change agents do a creditable job, it is because they've learned to bridge the gap between what management thinks it wants and what the rest of the company will buy. Needless to say, these staff people are worth their salt only when they outmanage management by triggering necessary changes before management realizes they are necessary.

Organization charts never show a box for change agents as such. Rather, they come disguised as industrial engineers, systems analysts, operations researchers, and so on. But, regardless of title or functional orientation, staff personnel working to analyze needs, plan changes, and then implement them are true change agents. They've become a necessary part of most larger companies because managing has become so complex that top-level change-oriented people are now needed on a full-time basis.

Is Your Company Ready for Change?

A company's change history will show whether it is ready for a particular kind of change. Some questions to consider are the following:

> Is the magnitude of this change too great to be acceptable?
> Are the company and its people sophisticated enough to make this change work?
> Is there a genuine need for the change?
> Is the timing right? Is the pace too fast? Is this change rate acceptable to the company?
> What is the company's tolerance for new thinking?

Careful consideration of these five points will determine whether a company can accept change. History may dictate that the change be shelved until the company is ready. But history is no more than a starting point. In time, people, markets, even entire companies gradually change their ways of thinking. The lesson to be learned is simply that a radical departure should not be expected unless the company itself has gone through a radical upheaval.

Knowing the company's change history, you're now prepared to develop an overall strategy as well as some specific tactics which, in the proper combination, will increase the chances of your success. Following are three tactics to consider in designing your strategy. (1) Knowing who's involved will help you decide which steps are appropriate. (2) Role playing is a painless way to test your idea. (3) Preselling change is a way of testing which way the wind is blowing before committing your forces. Let's look at each of these tactics in some depth.

Knowing who's involved. Change is normally accomplished through functions such as industrial engineering or through powerful individuals or committees. The magnitude of the change determines who is involved. For example, sweeping changes may emanate from the office of the president; minor changes, from staff people. But knowing the magnitude of your change and the organizational level involved won't necessarily tell you who in the department is the real decision maker. Department heads sometimes delegate decision making to someone familiar with the area affected by the suggested change. Vice presidents, for example, are often unfamiliar with the working details of their organizations, so they are certain to push the suggestion down to someone who can grapple with it. The lesson here is that most proposals are not likely to be evaluated by anyone in the top echelon of the organization. You can save considerable time and headache by finding out who the likely evaluator will be and then approaching him directly.

An evaluation assignment can be handed down in such a way as to kill a project before it is ever evaluated. For example, a staff evaluator receiving an assignment from a vice president with the words, "We're not interested in this, are we?" can hardly be expected to get on the bandwagon. Since key decision makers have trusted subordinates, find out who they are and get them involved in the change so it'll get the necessary support before it is launched.

Role playing. Part of planning change is planning

the presentation itself. It is at this point that your idea, succinctly written, pays off. Chances are that if we can put an idea down on paper, we can also explain it. And the first step in selling an idea is to communicate it. The best way to test your ability to communicate your ideas is to try out your presentation in a role-playing session. Let an associate or co-worker who knows nothing of the idea play the part of the decision maker. As you present your arguments he has to adopt a skeptical view, pick apart your presentation, and find reasons for rejecting your proposal. A rigorous role-playing situation should reveal flaws in your arguments and test your skill in communicating the ideas easily, without multiple explanations. In other words, it's a good workout before the main bout.

Role playing highlights the other elements in developing a change strategy. Just who are the decision makers you'll have to convince before your idea can get off the ground? What kinds of change have they bought in the past, and what caused them to buy? If you haven't already learned the answers, role playing will automatically force you to examine these critical areas. And role playing will help you decide whether to use a hard sell or a soft one for your audience. Remember that conservative promises are more likely to gain the confidence of intelligent minds, and such promises are easier to fulfill. The soft sell generally works well with thoughtful, analytical types. Importantly, a rigorous role-playing session may reveal that the best approach is to let your audience sell themselves by participating in a preliminary individual interview. Such sessions allow you to presell the change.

Preselling change. Changes require conditioning before they are finally accepted and should be pre-sold to people individually before they are presented to a group at large. This goes a long way to guarantee the final sale.

As a change agent alert to the need for change, you may determine that the time for change is at hand. But your opinion alone is not enough; your idea has to be tested in the marketplace. Fortunately, your marketplace is limited to the people in your company who ultimately have to subscribe to your ideas; no need to delve into consumer buying habits and spending patterns. Your ideas can be easily tested in one-to-one informal interviews. What is more, you'll be able to incorporate their invaluable ideas and thus get them to participate in the venture. Once they are participating, there is no question of acceptance and support.

Creative listening. The individual interview allows objections, if there are any, to come to the surface in a controlled environment. In a one-to-one conversation, objections can't infect others and snowball into a destructive session. Moreover, the one-to-one relationship allows you to listen creatively to the reasons behind the objections. Creative listening is going beyond the words to what is on the speaker's mind. Tone of voice, facial expression, and body language are clues to whether what the speaker says is what he means. If there is a discrepancy between what he says and what you think he means, ask fishing questions (see Chapter IV). Then by careful listening you can creatively merge his ideas into your proposal. The mere fact that a person has the opportunity to blow off steam could be valuable.

He may object for reasons other than the ones he'll give you. For example, his attitude toward the company may be negative because of some real or imagined threat to his security. Giving him a sympathetic hearing, regardless of what he says, will make him feel better about you and your ideas. It will also help you to understand what makes him tick, and such empathy will ultimately influence your proposals in ways that make sense from his standpoint.

Your ideas should be flexible enough so that through creative listening you can modify them to fit the needs you learn about in these conversations. Since each person you're preselling is an important part of your company his needs are an important part of the company's needs, provided that they don't conflict with the needs of others.

Few people really take the time to listen creatively. Most of us are so enamoured of our own ideas that we think they must be right for everyone. Good change agents learn to suppress their own egos and really listen to objections and the reasons behind them; then they adapt their own ideas and harness the ideas of others.

Selling Change Through Participation

So far your ideas have been based on an intimate knowledge of what your audience will buy. Individual preselling enables you to highlight the benefits of your ideas and get people thinking, but it may also give them time to mount their defense if they disagree with you. One strategy to avoid this is to present only enough of your proposal so they can understand the track you're on but not enough so they can shoot you down. The facts are a good beginning, but don't give them answers—let the answers come from them.

For example, in as objective a manner as you can, talk about a deplorable condition. If the condition you describe is sufficiently deplorable, your listeners will take one of two positions. The first position is defensive. If the condition you're talking about is under their jurisdiction, they'll hotly defend it and then justify it on the ground that it exists because of circumstances beyond their control or because it has always been done that way. The second position is passive. If the condition isn't under their direct control or if they just arrived on the scene they'll be less emotionally involved.

In the face of a defensive position you'll certainly have a fight on your hands if you attempt to pin down responsibility to any extent. When you have a fight on your hands regardless of the tactic you select, the less said, the better. That doesn't mean you'll retreat from the engagement; it means you'll let the person responsible describe how bad it is. All you have to do is pose a few questions that will encourage him to tell you all about it. Thus in an informal one-to-one relationship you can gain insights that would not be possible under more formal circumstances.

Now the focus of attention should be on future action. "What shall we do about it?" is the logical question. Set aside the reasons why a condition exists and concentrate on how to alter it. Placing blame does little good anyway; it just reinforces the defensive walls protecting those dedicated to perpetuating the status quo. The future is the time to make amends without stressing past mistakes, so concentrate on it. Smart change agents pave the way to change by gaining the participation of key decision makers or their subordinates, and they do this by focusing on the future in a one-to-one situation.

Working with individuals has other advantages. Approaching them one at a time gives you greater leeway in directing their thinking toward your goal, whereas a group can quickly get out of hand. Besides, a group has a tendency to ramble, and you'll waste a good deal of time in trying to direct their thoughts toward productive ends.

Although the idea of directing someone's thinking may seem sinister, it is simply a matter of focusing on a problem you've selected. The answers are never directed. Indeed, the changes that evolve may not even come close to what you envisioned before you began. Remember that the insights of others are bound to make the proposals better because they're the ones who live with the problems from day to day. The important thing is that once they are involved they have a stake in the outcome. The greater their involvement, the greater their stake.

Questions are the key to involvement, and good questions will guarantee heavy involvement. Beginning with the changes you envision, work backward to identify the conditions that caused you to see the necessity for change. For example, suppose you'd like to modify the order-processing system because customers have been complaining about late deliveries. An appropriate question under these circumstances would be: "How can we speed up deliveries to our customers?" The response may be what you expect or it may be completely unexpected. You have to be prepared for alternative solutions and at the same time be objective enough yourself to accept some new ideas. Anyone dealing in change has to be able to submerge his own ego enough to accept the ideas of others.

Answers to questions may reveal that facts surrounding your own ideas are faulty. Now is the time to find this out; not later, when your reputation is on the line. Misplaced facts or erroneous conclusions on your part are easily explained away at this time, before you are committed.

New data or new insights gathered from the questioning during an interview may cause a shift in strategy. Certainly they will modify the change to come. At this point in time, your strategy should be fluid and open to new emphasis or even a major shift in direction. The questioning and interview are really an extension of the fact gathering that caused you to develop your idea in the first place. This is important because it lets us try on ideas for size before committing ourselves to any specific idea. It allows us to modify our thoughts, incorporate the thoughts of others, and learn of and overcome objections in a give-and-take atmosphere.

Some Don'ts to Consider

So far we've looked at some things to do in developing a total change strategy. A few words of caution about the things that shouldn't be done are now in order. Let's consider two don'ts: Don't overplan and don't fall in love with your own ideas.

Don't overplan. Some changes require little planning; others require in-depth studies. All too often the ones that should have been given a practical trial are studied to death. Calling on a review board or sending a proposal to a committee for action is a certain way to strangle the best proposals quietly but not quickly, for nothing happens fast in committee. Some changes are evaluated and reevaluated until the costs incurred in the process are far more than the value of the change itself.

Instead of trying to cost each change to the penny, one company decided to have a preliminary review; if a change made any sense at all and didn't mess things up too badly, the company would try it and see what happened. This not only encouraged people to suggest changes but allowed the changes to be tested where it really counted—on the firing line and not on a committee's agenda.

Some changes, keyed to specific opportunities, are studied until long after the opportunities have passed. A crispness of action is vital here because of the change's timed nature, and the strategy selected should reflect this. When time is of the essence and you can't delicately maneuver a change, you'll just have to risk premature exposure and trust that your company's collective good judgment will win out.

Overplanning tends to freeze ideas and causes rigidity of thought that precludes the possibility of altering plans. Further, overplanning causes us to become emotionally attached to specific ideas because we've thought about them too long. There is a time for thinking and a time for action, and the two shouldn't be confused. Plan so that when people who participate in the detailed change are on the right track, you'll know it. Plan only to the degree necessary to guide the participants toward the desired objective. Keep plans fluid enough to allow wide latitude, but firm enough to stay on target.

Don't fall in love with your own ideas. Many excellent change ideas never get off the ground because the originators fall in love with their own ideas. After all, ideas are the creative output of a fertile mind and as such they are an extension of one's ego. If someone were to say in all seriousness that he didn't like your ideas it would have the same net effect as if he had said he didn't like you. Each is a form of rejection. Even people who are too polite to voice their opinions about our dress or speech habits will be vocal about our ideas, particularly if the ideas affect them.

There is nothing personal in this rejection, and it should be understood in that light; the rejection is directed at the idea, not the person. Adopting this kind of objective stance will give your idea the greatest chance for survival.

Making the Presentation

Many changes can be successfully accomplished by preselling one or two key people and not resorting to a formal group presentation. But some changes require the agreement of a larger group. Some or all of the group members may already have been presold, but their formal agreement in concert requires formal presentation. After all your preparation, the group's acceptance may seem to be a foregone conclusion. Don't be lulled into a false sense of security. The most critical step is just ahead.

At this point you may be so keyed up about the final presentation that the following statement will come as somewhat of a shock: If at all possible, don't have a formal presentation. You may enjoy the chance to expound on your idea, but it's doubtful whether your audience will feel quite the same way. Nothing can kill a new idea faster than exposing it to a group of people—even if they've already agreed to the idea in principle. Something comparable to mob psychology takes hold in a meeting of equals, and mobs lynch ideas fast. A strong leader may control a group, but you're taking a chance unless that leader is totally committed to the change.

Your preselling effort may have been successful. The people you talked to may have been most cooperative and even joined with you in developing reasonable alternatives. Yet when these same people get together in a group, each has his own particular domain to protect. Each wants to gain overall strength and lose as little power and authority as possible. When people say they are willing to change, what they really mean is that they are willing to trade off one advantage for another, but not willing to give up any unfair advantage they may already possess.

David J. Phillips humorously depicted the boardroom response to a new idea, as described by the secretary of the executive management committee:

They put Newey, she told him, right in the middle of the big oblong table, in the board room, around which the EMC met every other Wednesday, and stripped him of his Cautious Language right down to his bare facts (which seemed skimpy, she volunteered). A Methods and Procedures vice president knocked Newey's Reservations and Qualifications to the floor and the General Counsel kicked them under the table.

When Newey bent over to look for them, the Secretary related with a giggle, he was struck from behind with a well-aimed Entrenched Interest, and pitched forward, striking his head on the corner of a stainless steel Tradition, with which the board room was heavily ornamented. Before he could recover, the rest of the Committee was on him, led by the Comptroller wielding a knurled Budget. The Division Head tried to rush him to a Subcommittee for treatment and observation, but it was too late. Newey was interred quietly in the minutes that very afternoon.[2]

Such executive treatment explains the high mortality rate of new ideas and is reason enough to avoid group exposure.

Meeting Avoidance Techniques

If group presentations to gain final acceptance are dangerous, how then can change be sold? There are several paths to change that can work without formal meetings. The first is an informal meeting. More

[2] "The Death of Newey," *Business Management* (April 1972), p. 32.

agreements are reached in restaurants and cocktail lounges than conference rooms because results are often easier to attain in a relaxed environment away from the business and its pressures. If only a few key people have to agree to your change, have your individual interviews and then take them to lunch to discuss the problems you share in common. There may be a variety of things they want to discuss, but in the relaxed atmosphere of a quiet restaurant you can steer the discussion to something they've already agreed to.

But you don't have to run up a restaurant tab to sell. You can also get important agreements in a relatively short time by bringing presold managers together on some other neutral ground away from the office. State the purpose of the meeting and then leave it up to the others to come to their own conclusions. Since they've already been convinced they are likely to follow the ideas they've previously discussed with you. A little gentle steering on your part is all that's necessary.

Several other means of avoiding formal presentations can be used, but only if you're convinced a group meeting would not be productive. One tactic is to hold the individual preselling meetings, then assume acceptance of your change ideas, set the ball rolling, and put the burden on others to stop the change once it has begun. This tactic doesn't win friends, but if the change has already started it's hard for someone to turn back the clock.

Another tactic is to send out a memo to everyone concerned, spelling out the change in some detail. End the memo with the statement: "We'll implement this if we don't hear from you in a few days." By the time some people get around to reading their mail the change will be well on its way.

These ideas are based on the proposition that action speaks louder than words and doing something is better than doing nothing. They also take advantage of the fact that most people are too concerned with their own jobs to interfere with yours, and as long as a change has a minimal impact on them it will get through once the ball is rolling.

When Confrontation Is Inevitable

No matter how hard you try, some changes will have to be presented before a group. By now you may be wondering why we bother to presell a change if individual commitments will evaporate under group pressure. But if a proposal is to stand any chance at all it will be because we did presell. First, the idea will not be totally new to the audience. New ideas, because they are strange, tend to be rejected out of hand. Second, any sale is difficult enough as it is, and preselling can smooth the way. Third, there are bound to be those in a group who will subordinate their own interests to those of the company if they are convinced of an idea's overall merits.

Get group agreement. Convincing a group of the merits of a change depends on such factors as the proposal itself, how and where it is presented, your salesmanship, and enlisting the aid of key group members.

Base the change on need. It has been said that nothing can stop an idea whose time has come. Some companies are so ripe for change that no matter what kind is suggested, it will gain ready acceptance as long as it is remotely connected with the problems and holds some promise. Proposals should be timed to coincide with need. The ideal time to suggest a change is when one of two conditions exist: first, when the change is pertinent to a particular problem or opportunity the company is facing or will face in the immediate future; second, when the people who have to be convinced are ready to consider something new. If a company is faced with production difficulties, a plan to increase sales will not be enthusiastically received. Nor will it be easy to sell a change requiring large capital expenditures in a company faced with financial difficulties. Basing a change on need will focus attention on the benefits which make the change acceptable.

Make the change easy to accept. Changes requiring large commitments are hard to sell. And remember that commitments can include not only money but other resources in short supply, such as skilled manpower, equipment, and management time. Make your change easy to buy by making it small. You can often begin a program without fully committing your company's resources until you have tested its potential. It is usually easier to sell the idea of trying out a change because test results allow for a more intelligent decision later.

Reversible changes are easier to sell than irreversible ones. For example, changing a well-run manual order-processing system over to automated equipment is difficult to sell because the decision may be irreversible. Before the automated system can prove itself, the skilled manual system personnel may be gone. What does the company do if the system fails? A reversible change has the unique advantage of being sold on the ground that it can always be dropped if it doesn't work.

Split the proposal. Some change agents divide their proposals into two parts, a general one and a detailed one. The general proposal covers the change and the problem it is designed to solve or the opportunity it is to exploit. The detailed proposal explains why it is worth consideration, who will do it, how it can be accomplished, and when it should be done.

One reason for dividing a proposal into two parts is that the general proposal is relatively easy to sell because it sets the stage. Most people will agree, when presented with evidence, that a problem or opportunity exists. This makes the need for change obvious, and it is an easy transition to your recommendation. Your specific ideas may not be acceptable, and premature introduction of a detailed plan leaves little for anyone to do other than react negatively. But once you gain acceptance of your general plan, the details now directly affect your audience and can be worked out in conjunction with them. It is at this point that they will become involved in fleshing out the skeleton of the proposal. Once the ideas are theirs, the emphasis shifts from "Should we?" to "How should we?" The change is now sold in principle. Only the details remain to be worked out.

Some change proposals are made in such a way that they seem to say: "This is my idea; if you know what's good for you, you'll like it." Few people appreciate being backed into a corner in this way. They want to examine the change and feel they're a part of it. You can harness their desire to participate by getting them to talk about their ideas.

Benjamin Franklin once counseled would-be persuaders:

> The way to convince another is to state your case moderately and accurately. Then scratch your head, or shake it a little, and say that is the way it seems to you, but that of course, you may be mistaken about it; which causes your listener to receive what you have to say, and as like as not, turn about and try to convince you of it, since you are in doubt. But if you go at him in a tone of positiveness and arrogance you only make an opponent of him.

Heed Franklin's advice when you enlist the aid of key group members. If you know they're already convinced, ask them for their ideas during the meeting. When they endorse the change, the weight of their opinions is bound to influence others.

Change agents have to suppress their own egos to the point that they may not get credit for their proposals. The ideal situation is to get others so involved that they grab the idea, modify it to suit their needs, and then put it into practice. The change salesman can then take silent pride in having acted as the catalyst to get things rolling.

Use the word "we" in your presentation. Don't hog all the glory; spread it around. Give credit to those in the group who have strengthened your idea. Get them to point out the advantages. Arrange for someone in the group (ideally the most powerful man) to present part of the change. If you are not sure how well something will work, be frank about it. Don't oversell; understatements are easier to live with when you're trying to implement a change.

Listen to what the group is saying. Some change salesmen get so wrapped up in their own words that they forget to get reactions until it's all over. Listening will enable you to detect such subtleties as the way things are said, which will tell you a good deal about your audience's attitude toward your change.

The Sleeping Giant

A consultant change agent was called in to study the effectiveness of the research and development department in a medium-size company. It was apparent the department wasn't working very hard; over the years it had been neglected until it was just limping along, doing the minimum job but not much more. The problem wasn't internal to the department. Unwittingly everyone had neglected R&D's potential contribution and as a result the whole company was suffering. Clearly there was a need to use R&D's services to better advantage.

How do you wake up a company to the fact that it has been asleep at the switch? The change agent decided he needed the entire top management team to tackle this one, not simply for their brain power, although that could work to his advantage. Rather, he wanted them to participate in an awakening process; he wanted them to perceive the problem and get involved in its resolution at first hand. In that way, any evolved changes could be understood and more acceptable.

When the change agent made his presentation before the top management team he characterized R&D as a sleeping giant—a department with great potential that was waiting for someone to wake it up and put it to work.

During the presentation he offered some ideas as to how management could put the giant to work. As the meeting unfolded the ideas began to take hold, and that afternoon a wake-up program was launched. Although a lot of words were spoken that day it was the concept of a sleeping giant that alerted management to its new opportunities.

A presentation's style and language are key elements in its acceptance. Generally, the simpler the presentation the better. Sophisticated people are not insulted by simple language. If anything, it saves time by making ideas easier to grasp. Don't try to impress people with the size of your vocabulary; instead, strive for clarity with ordinary words put together with zip.

Don't take it for granted that the words you use mean the same to your listeners as they do to you. Use words that create vivid images to achieve clarity. Simple words and familiar images can be used to convey complex ideas. For example, the troops at Fort Benning learned about G.I. insurance during the Second World War when a staff captain gathered the men together, explained how the insurance worked, and then said, "O.K., line up here." Then everyone would get in line and sign up for insurance

One group of G.I.'s passing through Fort Benning consisted largely of mountain men with little formal education. When the captain told them about G.I. insurance and then said "line up," nobody budged because nobody understood "fiduciary concern" and "option" and all the other abstruse terms.

The captain turned the matter over to a second lieutenant who was a mountain man himself. He got the men together and told them, "Now, what did the man say? He said if you buy this insurance, and you go into action, and you get hit in the head with a bullet, they gotta pay your loved ones ten thousand clams. Now if you don't buy this insurance and you go into action and get hit in the head with a bullet, they don't gotta give your family nothin'. Now, it's no skin off my nose what you do. If you take it and you get killed, they pay your family ten thousand dollars. If you don't take it and you get killed, they send your family a ten pound box of nothin'. Now, who do you think they're gonna send into combat first?" They sold a lot of insurance at Fort Benning that day because the lieutenant knew his audience and knew how to get them to react.

Accentuate the Positive

Change, no matter how well conceived, can never be ideal. Each has to be a compromise between conflicting goals. All one can hope to do is to arrive at the best alternative that is acceptable to those who will have to live with the change. Because no change is perfect, there is a natural inclination to overemphasize its shortcomings. Once a group focuses on the negative features there is a tendency to do nothing. But procrastination may be a far worse alternative than the change, despite its negative features.

Similarly, some groups tend to dwell on remote possibilities. In attempting to explore every eventuality, they select a set of circumstances that could happen but in all probability will not. When measured against this remote possibility, the change may not seem well conceived. Although such explorations are well intentioned, they usually fail to consider how often such an event will in fact occur and how well your present procedures cover such exigencies.

Instead of dwelling on a change's negative features, its positive aspects should be highlighted. That is to say, the shortcomings should not be glossed over but should be used in a constructive way to strengthen your proposal.

For example, a change may require job skill levels different from those that are now being used in your organization. To solve this personnel problem you'll have to upgrade or downgrade existing personnel or hire new people. Because this change affects people there's a strong tendency to put it off indefinitely. But problems like this offer opportunities commensurate with the headaches. If greater skills are needed, skills training requires an investment but is obviously a positive course since it gives employees a chance to move upward. If lower skill levels are needed, the advantage is to the company and its supervisors because labor costs will be lower and it will be easier to hire and train less specialized personnel. Existing personnel could, in time, be made available for more important work.

166

Positive thinking can overcome objections, but its greatest benefit is in the mental attitude of the change agent himself. He won't waiver from his assigned path and will be forceful enough to convince those who are uncommitted that this indeed is a project worthy of their support. He will exude confidence and gain adherents through leadership based on broad participation and his knowledge of what has to be done.

Positive thinking can be used in other ways to help you sell change. Thinking positively means using imaginative ways to demonstrate the value of a change. For example, can benefits be illustrated dramatically with pictures? Words alone affect only the auditory senses; words and pictures have an impact on both auditory and visual senses. The combination may be just what you need.

Thinking positively also means getting excited. Visualize how much better off things will be when your change is adopted and put to work. Put this excitement into your presentation and it is bound to rub off on your listeners. Enthusiasm is contagious and can overcome a great deal of negative feelings; it has a magnetic quality that can draw support for your ideas.

The process of change is as old as time and as natural as the process of life, which is a constantly changing cycle. This obvious observation is necessary only as a counterpoint to the supposition that change in business is unnatural.

Business organizations themselves develop their own form of rigidity. They establish rules and procedures, lock themselves into repetitive patterns of behavior, and diminish their adaptability. Change is

167

natural; what is unnatural is for people to adhere to routine. Routine begets boredom, and organizations have to constantly struggle to keep their people alert and interested.

The problem is of course one of degree. Some routine is not only acceptable but mandatory for business to operate in a sensible manner. But overall, people like and seek a variety of experiences. If an employee doesn't derive the satisfaction of accomplishment from his job he will direct his energies elsewhere, and in the long run the company will suffer for his halfheartedness. For a person to function effectively, the work environment should be stable enough for him to have a place to stand steady but flexible enough for him to try new things at a rate both he and his company find comfortable.

In these times we are all caught up in the process of change either as change agents causing change to happen or as people affected by change that is triggered by some external force. We cannot stand on the sidelines as observers. It's better to be involved and on the side of productive change than to be uninvolved or against it, for time is on the side of the change agent. It's better to work your changes on others than to have others work their changes on you. The sidelines are not a safe place to hide. As change becomes the rule rather than the exception, it will be better to support meaningful change than to fight hopelessly to maintain the status quo. The ideas presented here can become the basis of a change strategy that will keep a company afloat in a sea of change.